CENTRE FOR HUMAN RIGHTS
Geneva

PROFESSIONAL TRAINING SERIES No. 4

National Human Rights Institutions

A Handbook on the
Establishment and Strengthening of National Institutions
for the Promotion and Protection of Human Rights

UNITED NATIONS
New York and Geneva, 1995

OBr 1278596

NOTE

The designations employed and the presentation of the material in this publication do not imply the expression of any opinion whatsoever on the part of the Secretariat of the United Nations concerning the legal status of any country, territory, city or area, or of its authorities, or concerning the delimitation of its frontiers or boundaries.

*
* *

Material contained in this publication may be freely quoted or reprinted, provided credit is given and a copy of the publication containing the reprinted material is sent to the Centre for Human Rights, United Nations, 1211 Geneva 10, Switzerland.

HR/P/PT/4

UNITED NATIONS PUBLICATION
Sales No. E.95.XIV.2 ISBN 92-1-154115-8
ISSN 1020-1688

The World Conference on Human Rights encourages the establishment and strenghthening of national institutions, having regard to the "Principles relating to the status of national institutions" and recognizing that it is the right of each State to choose the framework which is best suited to its particular needs at the national level.

VIENNA DECLARATION AND PROGRAMME OF ACTION

(Part I, para. 36)

FOREWORD

It is with great pleasure that I introduce this handbook, the fourth publication in the *Professional Training Series* launched by the United Nations Centre for Human Rights in 1994. Like the other publications in the series, the handbook is designed to complement the Centre's technical cooperation programme, while at the same time providing information and assistance to all those involved in developing the structures necessary to promote and protect human rights.

Human rights involve relationships among individuals, and between individuals and the State. The practical task of protecting human rights is, therefore, primarily a national one for which each State must be responsible. United Nations efforts to encourage the creation and strengthening of national human rights institutions can be traced back to 1946. However, it is only over the past few years that the international community has come to agreement as to the optimal structure and functioning of these bodies. A landmark in this process was the formulation of the Principles relating to the status of national institutions, which were endorsed by the General Assembly in 1993. The same year, the World Conference on Human Rights reaffirmed the important and constructive role played by national human rights institutions and called upon Governments to strengthen such bodies.

In the course of its work in the area of national institutions, the United Nations has come to realize that no single model of national institution can, or should be, recommended as the appropriate mechanism for all countries to fulfil their international human rights obligations. Although each country can benefit from the experience of others, national institutions must be developed taking into account cultural and legal traditions, as well as existing political organization.

The United Nations has also recognized that not all States eager to establish or strengthen national institutions have the necessary technical and financial capacity to do so. The Centre for Human Rights, under its technical cooperation programme, has provided expert and material assistance in this area to a number of countries in the past few years. The Centre encourages States to request assistance in building or strengthening national human rights institutions.

Human rights machinery of the kind which forms the subject-matter of this handbook cannot be expected to address all the human rights issues which are currently occupying governments and the international community. Nor are such institutions set up to replace the human rights organs of the United Nations or non-governmental organizations working in the same area. The role of national institutions is clearly complementary, and their strengthening can only enhance the effectiveness of both national and international systems for the promotion and protection of human rights.

José AYALA LASSO
United Nations High Commissioner
for Human Rights

ACKNOWLEDGEMENT

This handbook was prepared by the Technical Cooperation Branch of the United Nations Centre for Human Rights. Special thanks are due to those national institutions and private individuals who offered comments and suggestions on an earlier draft.

CONTENTS

ANNEXES

INTERNATIONAL INSTRUMENTS
cited in the present handbook

ABBREVIATION

Compilation Human Rights: A Compilation of International Instruments, vol. I (2 parts), *Universal Instruments* (United
Nations publication, Sales No. E.94.XIV.1)

Source

International Bill of Human Rights:

Universal Declaration of Human Rights	General Assembly resolution 217 A (III) of 10 December 1948; *Compilation*, p. 1.
International Covenant on Economic, Social and Cultural Rights	General Assembly resolution 2200 A (XXI) of 16 December 1966, annex; *Compilation*, p. 8.
International Covenant on Civil and Political Rights	General Assembly resolution 2200 A (XXI) of 16 December 1966, annex; *Compilation*, p. 20.
Optional Protocol to the International Covenant on Civil and Political Rights	General Assembly resolution 2200 A (XXI) of 16 December 1966, annex; *Compilation*, p. 41.
Second Optional Protocol to the International Covenant on Civil and Political Rights, aiming at the abolition of the death penalty	General Assembly resolution 44/128 of 15 December 1989, annex; *Compilation*, p. 46.
International Convention on the Elimination of All Forms of Racial Discrimination	General Assembly resolution 2106 A (XX) of 21 December 1965, annex; *Compilation*, p. 66.
Convention on the Elimination of All Forms of Discrimination against Women	General Assembly resolution 34/180 of 18 December 1979, annex; *Compilation*, p. 150.
Convention against Torture and Other Cruel, Inhuman or Degrading Treatment or Punishment	General Assembly resolution 39/46 of 10 December 1984, annex; *Compilation*, p. 293.

Convention on the Rights of the Child	General Assembly resolution 44/25 of 20 November 1989, annex; *Compilation*, p. 174.
International Convention on the Protection of the Rights of All Migrant Workers and Members of Their Families	General Assembly resolution 45/158 of 18 December 1990, annex; *Compilation*, p. 554.
Vienna Declaration and Programme of Action	Adopted by the World Conference on Human Rights, Vienna, 25 June 1993 (A/CONF.157/24 (Part I), chap. III).

GENERAL INTRODUCTION

A. Aims of the handbook

1. This handbook is based on the premise that strong and effective national institutions can contribute substantially to the realization of human rights and fundamental freedoms. As more countries take the decision to establish national human rights institutions, the need for guidelines on how such bodies can be created and operated for maximum effectiveness becomes increasingly evident.

2. Actual or potential strength and effectiveness are directly related to the legal mandate of the institution. A national institution which is rendered weak or ineffective by its constitutive law can increase its technical competence, but in the absence of legislative change it will never completely overcome its structural inadequacies. For this reason, the first target group of the handbook is Governments and other groups considering, or actually involved in, the planning process for the establishment of new institutions. For this group the handbook provides a summary of the various purposes for which a human rights institution may be established; an overview of elements necessary for its effective functioning; and a detailed analysis of the various responsibilities with which such an institution may appropriately be entrusted. Practical assistance in the drafting process is given in the form of legislative examples applicable to particular purposes, elements or responsibilities.

3. The second target group of the handbook is existing institutions, their establishing Governments and those involved in their operation. The strengthening of existing institutions can take a number of different forms. Governments may decide to improve an existing national institution by amending its founding legislation in order to provide for a broader mandate or otherwise increased powers. In such a situation the handbook can serve purposes similar to those outlined above in respect of institutions yet to be established. Of course, in the absence of such amendments, an existing institution must operate in accordance with the legislative framework within which it was created. In that case, the handbook may be used in order to maximize the effectiveness of those functions and powers with which the institution is vested.

4. The great differences in structure and functioning between existing national institutions clearly reflect cultural, political, historical and economic dissimilarities. For this reason, the handbook is not a blueprint for legislation. It is not prescriptive, and it does not set out to create a prototype or "ideal" institution against which the effectiveness of all others may be measured. There can be no model institution and there are no set rules. The user of this handbook will instead find a series of guidelines and recommendations based on a careful analysis of the achievements and difficulties of a wide range of institutions in many countries. Information in the handbook is also based on the results of conferences and meetings convened both within and outside the United Nations and on the experience gained by the United Nations Centre for Human Rights in providing technical assistance to Governments in this area. It should be noted that the Principles relating to the status of national institutions (the "Paris Principles"), which are discussed below (see paras. 25-27 and annex I), have been particularly important in this respect.

B. Organization of the handbook

5. Chapter I provides an overview of the historical and legal context within which present developments relating to national institutions are occurring. An introduction to the human rights system and the place of national institutions in that system is followed by a brief summary of United Nations activity in this field from 1946 to the present day. The problem of definition is then addressed and an outline provided of the features generally associated with the most common classifications: national commissions, specialized commissions and offices of the ombudsman.

6. Chapter II discusses the elements which may be considered necessary for the effective functioning of a national human rights institution and explains how these elements may be incorporated into the structure and operation of an institution for optimal effect.

7. Chapters III, IV and V are devoted to discussion of the three main tasks which national institutions may perform. Chapter III deals with promoting awareness and educating about human rights; chapter IV, with advising and assisting government; and chapter V, with investigating alleged human rights violations. In relation to each of the three tasks, information is provided on the various methods which can be adopted and the strategies which may be employed to maximize their effectiveness.

8. The handbook also includes a number of annexes. Annex I reproduces the Principles relating to the status of national institutions (see paras. 25-27 below). Annex II provides a list of contacts and resource points which may be of use to Governments and others involved in establishing a new institution or in strengthening an existing one. Annex III summarizes the technical cooperation programme of the United Nations Centre for Human Rights as it relates to national institutions. Annex IV reproduces the International Bill of Human Rights. A select bibliography includes mainly United Nations documents and other publications relating to national human rights institutions.

I. NATIONAL HUMAN RIGHTS INSTITUTIONS: BACKGROUND AND OVERVIEW

A. Human rights systems

9. National institutions are but one component of a complex, multi-level system which has been developed for the promotion and protection of human rights. The following paragraphs provide a brief overview of this system in order to illustrate the place of national institutions, and the functions and responsibilities with which they may appropriately be entrusted.

1. *The United Nations and human rights*

10. In the Preamble to the Charter of the United Nations, the peoples of the United Nations declare their determination "to save succeeding generations from the scourge of war . . . to reaffirm faith in fundamental human rights . . . and to promote social progress and better standards of life in larger freedom". Accordingly, Article 1 of the Charter proclaims that one of the purposes of the United Nations is to achieve international cooperation in promoting and encouraging respect for human rights and for fundamental freedoms for all without distinction as to race, sex, language or religion.

11. In the 45 years since the adoption of the Universal Declaration of Human Rights, the United Nations has developed a comprehensive strategy aimed at achieving the human rights objective set out in the Charter. The basis of this strategy is the body of international rules and standards which now cover virtually every sphere of human activity.

12. Upon this strong legislative foundation has been built an extensive network of human rights machinery designed further to develop international standards, to monitor their implementation, to promote compliance, and to investigate violations of human rights. The strategy is reinforced by a wide variety of public information activities and a technical cooperation programme designed to provide practical help to States in their efforts to promote and protect human rights.

13. These structures and activities permit the United Nations to play a pivotal standard-setting and leadership role in the struggle for human rights and fundamental freedoms. The task of promoting and protecting human rights, however, is not one which could or should be assumed by only one organization. United Nations practice in the field of human rights is based on the fundamental premise that universal respect for human rights requires the concerted efforts of every Government, every individual, every group and every organ in society.

2. *Regional human rights systems*

14. The international system relies heavily on the support it receives from regional human rights systems such as those operating in Africa, the Americas and Europe. Regional human rights systems have played an important complementary role in reinforcing international standards and machinery by providing the means by which human rights concerns can be addressed within the particular social, historical and political context of the region concerned.

3. *Non-governmental organizations*

15. Additional support for implementation of international human rights standards comes from concerned community and non-governmental organizations, which have a special role to play in the development of a universal culture of human rights. Non-governmental organizations, by their very nature, have a freedom of expression, a flexibility of action and a liberty of movement which, in certain circumstances, allow them to perform tasks which Governments and intergovernmental organizations are unable or even unwilling to perform.

4. *Governments*

16. In the past two decades many countries have become parties to the major human rights treaties, thereby incurring a legal obligation to implement the human rights standards to which they subscribe at the international level. Human rights involve relationships among individuals, and between individuals and the State. The practical task of protecting human rights is therefore primarily a national one, for which each State must be responsible. At the national level, rights can be best protected through adequate legislation, an independent judiciary, the enactment and enforcement of individual safeguards and remedies, and the establishment and strengthening of democratic institutions. Activities aimed at the promotion of human rights and the development of a human rights culture should also be viewed as primarily national responsibilities. The most effective education and information campaigns, for example, are likely to be those which are designed and carried out at the national or local level and which take the local cultural and traditional context into account.

17. When States ratify a human rights instrument, they either incorporate its provisions directly into their domestic legislation or undertake to comply in other ways with the obligations contained in the instrument. Therefore, universal human rights standards and norms today find their expression in the domestic laws of most countries. Often, however, the fact that a law exists to protect certain rights is not enough if that law does not also provide for all the legal powers and institutions necessary to ensure the effective realization of those rights.

18. This problem of effective implementation at the national level has, particularly in recent times, generated a great deal of international interest and action. The emergence or reemergence of democratic rule in many countries has focused attention on the importance of

democratic institutions in safeguarding the legal and political foundations on which human rights are based.

19. It has therefore become increasingly apparent that the effective enjoyment of human rights calls for the establishment of national infrastructures for their promotion and protection. In recent years, many countries have established institutions with the express function of protecting human rights. While the specific tasks of such institutions may vary considerably from country to country, they share a common purpose, and for this reason are referred to collectively as national human rights institutions.

B. United Nations activity in the area of national institutions

1. Early activities of the Economic and Social Council

20. The question of national human rights institutions was first discussed by the Economic and Social Council (ECOSOC) in 1946, two years before the General Assembly proclaimed the Universal Declaration of Human Rights as "a common standard of achievement for all peoples and all nations".

21. At its second session, in 1946, ECOSOC invited Member States "to consider the desirability of establishing information groups or local human rights committees within their respective countries to collaborate with them in furthering the work of the Commission on Human Rights".[1] Fourteen years later the matter was raised again, in a resolution which recognized the important role national institutions could play in the promotion and protection of human rights, and which invited Governments to encourage the formation and continuation of such bodies as well as to communicate all relevant information on the subject to the Secretary-General.[2] This process is an ongoing one, and reports on information received are regularly submitted by the Secretary-General to the Commission on Human Rights, to the General Assembly and to States.

2. Establishing standards and goals for national institutions

22. As standard-setting in the field of human rights gained momentum during the 1960s and 1970s, discussions on national institutions became increasingly focused on the ways in which such bodies could assist in the effective implementation of these international standards. In 1978, the Commission on Human Rights decided to organize a seminar in order, *inter alia*, to draft guidelines for the structure and functioning of national institutions. Accordingly, the Seminar on National and Local Institutions for the Promotion and Protection of Human Rights was held in Geneva in September 1978[3]

and approved a set of such guidelines. These guidelines suggested that the functions of national institutions should be:

To act as a source of human rights information for the Government and people of the country;

To assist in educating public opinion and promoting awareness of and respect for human rights;

To consider, deliberate upon and make recommendations regarding any particular state of affairs that may exist nationally and which the Government may wish to refer to them;

To advise on any questions regarding human rights matters referred to them by the Government;

To study and keep under review the status of legislation, judicial decisions and administrative arrangements for the promotion of human rights, and to prepare and submit reports on these matters to the appropriate authorities;

To perform any other function which the Government may wish to assign to them in connection with the duties of the State under those international instruments in the field of human rights to which it is a party;

As regards the structure of such institutions; the guidelines recommended that they should:

Reflect in their composition wide cross-sections of the nation, thereby bringing all parts of the population into the decision-making process in regard to human rights;

Function regularly, and that immediate access to them should be available to any member of the public or any public authority;

In appropriate cases, have local or regional advisory organs to assist them in discharging their functions.

23. The guidelines were subsequently endorsed by the commission on Human Rights and the General Assembly. The Assembly invited States to take appropriate steps for the establishment, where they did not already exist, of national institutions for the promotion and protection of human rights, and requested the Secretary-General to submit a detailed report on existing national institutions.

24. Throughout the 1980s, the United Nations continued to take an active interest in this topic and a series of reports prepared by the Secretary-General was presented to the General Assembly. It was during this time that a considerable number of national institutions were established—many with the support of the United Nations Centre for Human Rights

3. The 1991 first international meeting in Paris

25. In 1990, the Commission on Human Rights called for a workshop ro be convened with the participation of national and regional institutions involved in the promotion and protection of human rights. The workshop was to review patterns of cooperation between national institutions and international organizations, such as the United Nations and its agencies, and to explore ways of increasing the effectiveness of national institu-

---

[1] Economic and Social Council resolution 2/9 of 21 June 1946, sect. 5.

[2] Economic and Social Council resolution 772 B (XXX) of 25 July 1960.

[3] See ST/HR/SER.A/2 and Add.1.

tions. Accordingly, the first International Workshop on National Institutions for the Promotion and Protection of Human Rights was held in Paris from 7 to 9 October 1991.[4] Its conclusions were endorsed by the Commission on Human Rights in resolution 1992/54 as the Principles relating to the status of national institutions (the "Paris Principles"), and subsequently by the General Assembly in its resolution 48/134 of 20 December 1993. The principles affirm that national institutions are to be vested with competence to promote and protect human rights and given as broad a mandate as possible, set forth clearly in a constitutional or legislative text.

26.   According to these Principles, which represent a refinement and extension of the guidelines developed in 1978 (see para. 22 above) a national institution shall, *inter alia*, have the following responsibilities:

To submit recommendations, proposals and reports on any matter relating to human rights (including legislative and administrative provisions and any situation of violation of human rights) to the Government, parliament and any other competent body;

To promote conformity of national laws and practices with international human rights standards;

To encourage ratification and implementation of international standards;

To contribute to the reporting procedure under international instruments;

To assist in formulating and executing human rights teaching and research programmes and to increase public awareness of human rights through information and education;

To cooperate with the United Nations, regional institutions, and national institutions of other countries.

The Principles also recognized that a number of national institutions have been given competence to receive and act on individual complaints of human rights violations. They stipulate that the functions of national institutions in this respect may be based on the following principles:

Seeking an amicable settlement of the matter through conciliation, binding decision or other means;

Informing the complainant of his or her rights and of available means of redress, and promoting access to such redress;

Hearing complaints or referring them to a competent authority;

Making recommendations to the competent authorities, including proposals for amendment of laws, regulations or administrative practices which obstruct the free exercise of rights.

27.   The Principles also include detailed guidelines on the composition of national institutions and the appointment of members; on guarantees of independence and pluralism; and on methods of operation. The full text

of the Principles is reproduced in annex I to this handbook and their spirit is reflected in the guidelines and recommendations made below.

4. *Activities during 1991-1993*

28.   Since 1991, the work of the United Nations in relation to national institutions has gained considerable momentum. A number of important meetings have been convened, including the Second United Nations Workshop for the Asian and Pacific Region on Human Rights Issues (Jakarta, January 1993),[5] at which the establishment of national institutions in the Asian and Pacific region was discussed; the meeting of Representatives of National Institutions and Organizations Promoting Tolerance and Harmony and Combating Racism and Racial Discrimination (Sydney, April 1993);[6] and the second International Workshop on National Institutions for the Promotion and Protection of Human Rights (Tunis, December 1993).[7]

5. *The 1993 World Conference on Human Rights*

29.   During preparations for the 1993 World Conference on Human Rights, it was decided to organize a meeting of national institutions parallel to the Conference itself. This meeting examined, *inter alia*, the purposes of national institutions; the key requisites for appropriate and effective functioning, including representative nature and accessibility; and mechanisms for coordinating inter-institutional activities.

30.   The Vienna Declaration and Programme of Action adopted by the World Conference confirmed many important principles, including that of the indivisibility and interdependence of all human rights, as well as establishing an ambitious agenda for human rights into the twenty-first century. With regard to national institutions, the World Conference reaffirmed therein:

... the important and constructive role played by national institutions for the promotion and protection of human rights, in particular in their advisory capacity to the competent authorities, their role in remedying human rights violations, in the dissemination of human rights information, and education in human rights. ... (Part I, para. 36.)

It also encouraged:

... the establishment and strengthening of national institutions, having regard to the "Principles relating to the status of national institutions" ... (Ibid.)

and recognized:

... the right of each State to choose the framework which is best suited to its particular needs at the national level. (Ibid.)

31.   The World Conference also called upon Governments to strengthen national institutions; recommended the strengthening of United Nations activities and programmes to meet requests for assistance from States in the establishment or strengthening of national institutions; encouraged cooperation between national institutions, particularly through exchanges of information and experience, as well as through cooperation with

---

[4] See E/CN.4/1992/43 and Add.1.

[5] See HR/PUB/93/1

[6] See A/CONF.157/PC/92/Add.5.

[7] See E/CN.4/1994/45 and Add.1.

regional organizations and the United Nations; and recommended, in that regard, that periodic meetings be convened between representatives of national institutions, under the auspices of the Centre for Human Rights, in order to share experience and examine ways and means of improving their mechanisms.

6. *The 1993 second international meeting at Tunis*

32. The second International Workshop on National Institutions for the Promotion and Protection of Human Rights was held at Tunis from 13 to 17 December 1993,[8] and brought together representatives of more than 28 institutions from around the world. Workshop participants discussed a number of topics of mutual concern, including relations between the State and national institutions, between national institutions themselves, and between national institutions and the Centre for Human Rights. As part of an effort to improve cooperative relationships, the workshop formally established a Coordinating Committee (see para. 115 below). It also adopted a number of recommendations, including one which called upon individual institutions to take measures to ensure that their status and activities are consistent with the Paris Principles relating to the status of national institutions (see paras. 25-27 above).

7. *Activities outside the United Nations system*

33. Several international organizations, particularly the Commonwealth Secretariat and the International Ombudsman Institute, have been active in promoting the establishment and development of national human rights institutions.

34. The Commonwealth has sponsored a number of international and national workshops and has developed extensive materials. These include a directory of existing institutions in Commonwealth countries and a manual which provides comparative legislation and guidance for States wishing to establish new institutions.

35. The International Ombudsman Institute has, in recent years, paid increasing attention to the human rights dimension of the work of ombudsmen. The Institute, located in Alberta, Canada, gathers information on all ombudsman offices throughout the world and, through publications and conferences, attempts to strengthen relations between individual institutions.

C. Defining a national human rights institution

36. Despite the existence of comprehensive standards relating to practice and to functions, an analysis of activities conducted both within and outside the United Nations system reveals that there is not yet an agreed definition of the term "national human rights institution". The conceptual framework for early United Nations activities in the area was flexible enough to include virtually any institution at the national level having a direct or indirect impact on the promotion and protection of human rights. Accordingly, the judiciary, administra-

tive tribunals, legislative organs, non-governmental organizations, legal aid offices and social welfare schemes were all given equal attention, along with national commissions, ombudsman offices and related structures.

37. This broad formulation, however, has been gradually pared down by the subsequent work of the United Nations on the subject to the point where a more narrow group of institutions has emerged, on the basis of particular common functions, including: educational and promotional activities; the provisions of advice to government on human rights matters; and the investigation and resolution of complaints of violations committed by public (and occasionally also private) entities. However, while operating to exclude previously included institutions such as the judiciary, the legislature and social welfare structures, this "functional" approach to categorization has not yet resulted in an ultimate definition of what constitutes a national institution for the promotion and protection of human rights.

38. The Paris Principles relating to the status of national institutions (see paras. 25-27 above) represent an important step in the evolutionary process. The Principles attempt to clarify the concept of a "national institution" by providing standards on the status and advisory role of national human rights commissions. If these standards are applied to the general class of national institutions, not only those designated as "commissions", then a national institution must be a body established in the constitution or by law to perform particular functions in the field of human rights. This process will then operate to exclude not only governmental instrumentalities with more general functions (such as administrative tribunals), but also all organizations not founded in law.

39. Despite these refinements, it is evident that the concept of a national institution is not yet fully evolved. At the same time, the practical utility of establishing boundaries, however flexible, has been recognized. For the purposes of United Nations activities in this field, therefore, the term "national institution" is taken to refer to a body which is established by a Government under the constitution, or by law or decree, the functions of which are specifically defined in terms of the promotion and protection of human rights.

D. National institutions in practice

40. In practice, the institutions included in the above definition are all "administrative" in nature—in the narrow sense that they are neither "judicial" nor lawmaking. As a rule, they are endowed with ongoing, advisory authority in respect of human rights at the national and/or international level. These purposes are pursued either in a general way, through opinions and recommendations, or through the consideration and resolution of complaints submitted by individuals or groups. In some countries, the constitution will provide for the establishment of a national human rights institution. More often, such institutions are created by legislation or decree. While many national institutions are attached, in some way or another, to the executive branch of government, the actual level of independence which they enjoy will depend on a number of factors, including

---

[8] Ibid.

composition, financial basis and the manner in which they operate.

1. *Classification difficulties*

41. The existence of such common characteristics has not prevented significant classification difficulties. At present, the majority of national institutions are identified as belonging to one of two broad categories: "human rights commissions" or "ombudsmen".

42. Human rights commissions are generally involved in one more specific functions directly related to the promotion and protection of human rights, including an advisory function (with regard to law and government policy on human rights), an educative function (oriented towards the public), and what may be termed an impartial investigatory function. Differences between various commissions are often related to differences in the weight given to particular functions. The focus of a commission may range across a broad spectrum of rights or, conversely, may be restricted to protection of a particular vulnerable group.

43. From a comparative perspective, the institution of ombudsman is generally associated with an emphasis on the impartial investigatory function. Many long-established offices of the ombudsman do not concern themselves directly with human rights except in so far as they relate to their principal function of overseeing fairness and legality in public administration. Others, particularly the more recently created offices, have been given specific human rights protection mandates, often in relation to rights set forth in national constitutions or other legislation.

44. Despite the existence of such indicators, precise classification of a particular institution is complicated by the fact that functions implied in these designations are not always reflected in the work of institutions so categorized. An "ombudsman", for example, may be engaged in a broad range of promotional and protective activities generally recognized as characteristic of a commission. An entity identified as a "human rights commission" may be operating exclusively within the sphere of public administration—a domain traditionally associated with the office of the ombudsman.

45. In view of such inconsistencies, it is clear that any attempt at nominal classification will be somewhat arbitrary and that a functional approach to defining national institutions may be more appropriate. it is in accordance with such a functional approach that the substantive parts of this handbook have been organized. However, as distinctions and categorizations continue to exist in practice, they cannot be ignored. In providing an overview of existing national institutions, the following sections outline the features, generally associated with national commissions, specialized commissions and offices of the ombudsman.

2. *Human rights commissions*

46. In many countries, commissions have been established to ensure that the laws and regulations concerning the protection of human rights are effectively applied. Most human rights commissions function

independently of other organs of government, although they may be required to report to the legislature on a regular basis.

47. In keeping with their independent nature, commissions are generally composed of a variety of members from diverse backgrounds, each with a particular interest, expertise or experience in the field of human rights. Each country may have its specific requirements or restrictions for the selection of members, such as quotas on the number of representatives or candidates from various professional categories, political parties or localities.

48. Human rights commissions are concerned primarily with the protection of persons against all forms of discrimination and with the protection of civil and political rights. They may also be empowered to promote and protect economic, social and cultural rights. The precise authority and functions of a particular commission will be defined in the legislative act or decree under which it is established. This law or decree will also serve to define the commission's jurisdiction by, *inter alia*, specifying the range of discriminatory or violative conduct which it is empowered to investigate or otherwise act on. Some commissions concern themselves with alleged violations of any rights recognized in the constitution. Others may be able to consider cases of discrimination on a broad range of grounds, including race, religion, gender, national or ethnic origin, disability, social condition, sexual orientation, political opinion, ancestry, age and marital status.

49. One of the most common functions vested in a human rights commission is to receive and investigate complaints from individuals (and, occasionally, from groups) alleging human rights abuses committed in violation of existing national law. In order to carry out its tasks properly, the commission will usually be capable of obtaining evidence relating to the matter under investigation. Even if used only rarely, this power is important in that it guards against the possibility of frustration through lack of cooperation on the part of the person or body complained against. While there are considerable differences in the procedures followed by various human rights commissions in the investigation and resolution of complaints, many rely on conciliation and/or arbitration. In the process of conciliation, the commission will attempt to bring the two parties together in order to achieve a mutually satisfactory outcome. If conciliation fails to resolve the dispute, the commission may be able to resort to arbitration in which it will, after a hearing, issue a determination.

50. It is not common for a human rights commission to be granted authority to impose a legally binding outcome on parties to a complaint. However, this does not mean that the settlement or appropriate remedial steps recommended by the commission can be ignored. In some cases, a special tribunal will hear and determine issues outstanding from an unresolved complaint. If no special tribunal has been established, the commission may be able to transfer unresolved complaints to the regular courts for a final and binding determination.

51. Another important function of many commissions is systematically to review the Government's hu-

man rights policy in order to detect shortcomings in human rights observance and suggest ways of improving it. Human rights commissions may also monitor the State's compliance with its own legislation and with international human rights laws and, if necessary, recommend changes. The ability of a commission to initiate inquiries on its own behalf is an important measure of its overall strength and probable effectiveness. This is particularly true in regard to situations involving persons or groups who do not have the financial or social resources to lodge individual complaints.

52. The full realization of human rights cannot be achieved solely through adequate legislation and appropriate administrative arrangements. In recognition of this fact, commissions are often entrusted with the important responsibility of improving community awareness of human rights. Promoting and educating about human rights may involve informing the public about the commission's own functions and purposes; provoking discussion about various important questions in the field of human rights; organizing seminars and training courses; arranging counselling services and meetings; and producing and disseminating human rights publications.

3. Specialized institutions

53. Vulnerable groups differ from country to country, but the most common problem affecting them all is discrimination. Members of the community who are most often recognized by Governments as needing specialized human rights bodies to protect their interests are persons belonging to ethnic, linguistic and religious minorities, indigenous populations, non-nationals, migrants, immigrants, refugees, children, women, the poor and the disabled.

54. Specialized human rights institutions are generally established to promote government and social policy which has been developed for the protection of one or more of these groups. For the most part, these institutions perform functions similar to those of the less specific human rights commissions described above. They are usually authorized to investigate instances and patterns of discrimination against individuals in the group and against the group as a whole. While generally able to investigate complaints brought by a member of the group against another person or against a government body, these specialized institutions are, like other national human rights institutions, rarely empowered to make binding decisions or to initiate legal action.

55. As well as providing material and consultative assistance on an individual and collective basis, such institutions will frequently be responsible for monitoring the effectiveness of existing laws and constitutional provisions as these relate to the group. In this way, they often act as consultants and advisers to parliament and the executive branch of government.

4. The ombudsman

56. The office of ''ombudsman'' is now established in a wide range of countries, some of which use other designations to describe institutions in this category, such as Avocat du peuple, Defensor del Pueblo,

Médiateur de la République, etc. The ombudsman (who is often one person but may also be a group of persons) is generally appointed by the parliament acting on constitutional authority or through special legislation. However, in parts of Africa and the Commonwealth, the ombudsman's appointment is the responsibility of the head of State, to whom the institution may also be required to report.

57. The primary function of this institution is to oversee fairness and legality in public administration. More specifically, the office of the ombudsman exists to protect the rights of individuals who believe themselves to be the victim of unjust acts on the part of the public administration. Accordingly, the ombudsman will often act as an impartial mediator between an aggrieved individual and the Government.

58. While the institution of ombudsman is not exactly the same in any two countries, all follow similar procedures in the performance of their duties. The ombudsman receives complaints from members of the public and will investigate these complaints provided they fall within the ombudsman's competence. In the process of investigation, the ombudsman is generally granted access to the documents of all relevant public authorities and may also be able to compel witnesses, including government officials, to provide information. He or she will then issue a statement or recommendation based on this investigation. This statement is generally transmitted to the person lodging the complaint as well as to the office or authority complained against. In general, if the recommendation is not acted on, the ombudsman may submit a specific report to the legislature. This will be in addition to an annual report to the same body, which may include information on problems which have been identified and contain suggestions for legislative and administrative change.

59. While any citizen who believes that his or her rights have been violated may submit a complaint to the ombudsman, many countries require that the complainant first exhaust all alternative legal and administrative remedies. There may also be time-limits imposed on the filing of complaints. Moreover, while the ombudsman's authority usually extends to all aspects of public administration, most ombudsmen are prevented from considering complaints involving members of the legislature or the judiciary.

60. Access to the ombudsman also varies from country to country. In many countries, individuals may lodge a complaint directly with the ombudsman's office. In other countries, complaints may be submitted through an intermediary, such as a local member of parliament. Complaints made to the ombudsman are usually confidential, and the identity of the complainant is not disclosed without that person's consent.

61. The ombudsman is not always restricted to acting on complaints and may be able to begin an investigation on his or her own initiative. As with human rights commissions, self-initiated investigations by ombudsman offices often relate to issues which the ombudsman may have determined to be of broad public concern, or

issues which affect group rights and are therefore not likely to be the subject of an individual complaint.

62. In many respects, the powers of the ombudsman are quite similar to those of human rights commissions with competence to receive and investigate complaints. Both are concerned with protecting the rights of individuals and, in principle, neither has the power to make binding decisions. There are nevertheless some differences in the functions of the two bodies which reveal why some countries establish and simultaneously maintain both types of institution. As explained above, the primary function of most ombudsmen is to ensure fairness and legality in public administration. In contrast,

commissions are more generally concerned with violations of human rights, particularly discrimination. In this respect, human rights commissions will often concern themselves with the actions of private bodies and individuals as well as of the Government. In general, the principal focus of activity for an ombudsman is individual complaints against public entities or officials. However, distinctions are becoming more and more blurred as ombudsman offices engage in a wider range of activities for the promotion and protection of human rights. Increasingly, offices of the ombudsman are assuming responsibilities in the area of promoting human rights, particularly through educational activities and the development of information programmes.

II. ELEMENTS FOR THE EFFECTIVE FUNCTIONING OF NATIONAL INSTITUTIONS

A. Introduction

63. The Vienna Declaration and Programme of Action adopted by the 1993 World Conference on Human Rights specifically recognized the right of each State to choose the framework for a national human rights institution which is best suited to its needs (see para. 30 *in fine* above). This provision represents a clear acknowledgement of the fact that the great differences which exist between States will necessarily be reflected in the structures which they create to implement international human rights standards.

64. As pointed out earlier (para. 4 above), it is not the purpose of this handbook to ignore essential differences and to promote a prototype or model institution. Instead, its principal objective is to encourage and facilitate the development of appropriate and effective institutions. "Appropriateness" may be evaluated by reference to the extent to which the structure of a particular national institution takes account of national conditions and circumstances, including political, cultural and economic realities. "Effectiveness", on the other hand, can only ever be measured by reference to the extent to which a national institution positively affects the human rights situation of individuals and groups in a given society.

65. Appropriateness is a prerequisite for effectiveness. An inappropriate institution (in terms of jurisdiction, powers, or any other measures) will be an ineffective one. It is difficult, and perhaps not particularly useful, to lay down one set of rules for developing an appropriate institution. The present chapter will therefore not deal with the issue of appropriateness except to provide general guidelines within specific contexts. In their efforts to establish and develop appropriate, relevant institutions, States will benefit from the experience of others, particularly those in geographical, political, economic or cultural proximity.

66. The primary purpose of this chapter, therefore, is to identify those elements which may be considered essential to the effective functioning of national institutions. The basic differences which exist between States and between institutions make it both difficult and unwise to formulate inflexible guidelines for ensuring effectiveness. Nevertheless, the fact remains that, by definition, all national institutions share certain common goals. This commonality of objectives permits the following "effectiveness factors" to be identified as generally applicable:

Independence;

Defined jurisdiction and adequate powers;

Accessibility;

Cooperation;

Operational efficiency;

Accountability.

67. This chapter is divided into six further sections, each devoted to consideration of one of the elements set out above. In each section, an analysis is made of the way in which the subject factor can influence the effective functioning of a national institution. This analysis is followed by an examination of the mechanisms by which the element can be incorporated into both the structure and functioning of a national institution.

B. Independence

68. An effective national institution will be one which is capable of acting independently of government, of party politics and of all other entities and situations which may be in a position to affect its work. Independence is, however, a relative concept. The very fact that a national institution is granted a certain independence of action distinguishes it from government instrumentalities. On the other hand, independence for a national institution can never mean a total lack of connection to the State. The definition of a national institution includes the requirement that it be established by law. The founding law of a national institution will identify specific links with the State and define the limits within which the institution is to function. All institutions are necessarily restricted by their links with the State and by the need to conform to their legislative mandates. Other realities precluding full independence include reporting obligations and a lack of full financial autonomy. It is, in fact, this legislative basis, and the restrictions which accompany it, which distinguish a national institution from a non-governmental organization.

69. At best, therefore, a national institution will enjoy a measure of qualified independence the implication of which must be considered contextually. The following discussion is based on the view that it is the functions of a national institution which are important in this regard. While the establishment of every institution will necessitate the imposition of certain limitations, restrictions on independence should not be such as to interfere with the ability of an institution to discharge its responsibilities effectively.

1. *Independence through legal and operational autonomy*

70. The founding law of a national institution will be critical in ensuring its legal independence, particularly its independence from government. Ideally, a national institution will be granted separate and distinct legal personality of a nature which will permit it to exercise independent decision-making power. Independent legal status should be of a level sufficient to permit an institution to perform its functions without interference or obstruction from any branch of government or any public or private entity. This may be achieved by making the institution directly answerable to parliament

International Convention on the Protection of the Rights of All Migrant Workers and Members of Their Families (not yet in force; committee not yet established).

Reports generally contain information concerning the national situation with regard to a particular right or set of rights protected by the relevant instrument. They will also include details of the ways in which the reporting State is working towards implementing its international obligations. Each Committee is composed of a number of experts who examine individual reports, question State representatives and make either specific or general recommendations concerning ways in which rights may be implemented at the national level. An accurate, detailed and properly drafted report will ensure that the submitting State receives maximum benefit from the expertise of the Committee.

212.   Increasingly, State parties' reports to the various committees are including information on the activities of national institutions in so far as these activities relate to the area covered by the report. A national human rights institution is, by definition, itself an implementation mechanism and for that reason an appropriate subject for inclusion in reports. The institution will assume even greater prominence in a report where its activities directly relate to the rights in question. A national institution dealing with the problem of racial discrimination, for example, will presumably be conducting activities relevant to implementation of the State's obligations under the International Convention on the Elimination of All Forms of Racial Discrimination. The Committee on the Rights of the Child may be expected to receive information from States parties on the existence and functioning of any national institutions which are directly involved in promoting and protecting the human rights of children.

213.   In addition to being the subject of part of a report, a national institution may be able to contribute to the reports which States are required to submit to United Nations bodies and committees, and to regional institutions, pursuant to their treaty obligations. The importance of accurate, detailed and properly drafted reports has already been stressed. National institutions, by virtue of their particular expertise, are often in an excellent position to ensure that reports conform in these three important respects.

214.   The contributions of national institutions to the reporting process will vary according to a number of factors, including the functions of an institution and the willingness of the Government to seek its assistance. In many cases, a national institution will be able to offer information, data or statistics directly to the government department charged with preparing the report. Some institutions may review draft reports in order to ensure their accuracy and completeness. Others may be used as a coordinating point through which information from various ministries, departments and organizations is channelled. In this latter case, a national institution itself may be entrusted with the responsibility of compiling a draft report, which would then be submitted to the relevant authorities for review.

3. Assisting in the development of national action plans

215.   In the 1993 Vienna Declaration and Programme of Action (Part II, para. 71), the World Conference on Human Rights recommended that each State consider the desirability of drawing up a national action plan identifying steps whereby that State would improve the promotion and protection of human rights. In developing their respective action plans, States will be required to set priorities in the field of human rights as well as to identify the appropriate vehicles through which the plan is to be implemented. In recognition of their expertise and experience, national institutions should be recruited to assist in the drafting of action plans and utilized as much as possible in the implementation process.

V. THE TASK OF INVESTIGATING ALLEGED HUMAN RIGHTS VIOLATIONS

A. Introduction

216. One of the most important functions with which a national human rights institution can be entrusted is the investigation of alleged human rights violations. The existence of a national mechanism with the power to investigate abuses and provide relief to victims can act as a powerful disincentive to violative behaviour. It is also a clear indication of a Government's commitment to human rights and of its genuine willingness to take international and domestic obligations seriously.

217. An effective investigatory mechanism will be characterized by:

Adequate legal capacity;

Organizational competence;

A defined and appropriate set of priorities;

The political will to pursue its work.

This chapter focuses principally on the first two of these four basic requirements. The setting of priorities and the existence of the necessary political will, while referred to incidentally, are matters which must be addressed and resolved within each society and each institution. However, with regard to the latter point, it should be stressed at the outset that an investigatory mechanism cannot function properly without a certain measure of support from the Government. Experience has repeatedly shown that, regardless of legal powers, a mechanism which does not enjoy such support will not be able to operate effectively.

218. This chapter has two main sections. Section B deals with the structure and functioning of mechanisms for receiving, acting on and resolving complaints from individuals and groups. Section C examines the procedure for investigating human rights situations *suo moto*, i.e. at the institution's own initiative and not on the basis of a complaint received.

B. Investigating complaints

1. *Importance of a complaints mechanism*

219. The judiciary is the basic structure for protection of human rights at the national level. A national human rights institution, no matter how wide the powers or efficient its operation, can never adequately substitute for a properly functioning judiciary.

220. The ability of a national institution to receive and act on complaints should therefore be seen as an additional measure of security—a complementary mechanism established to ensure that the rights of all citizens are fully protected. This complementarity implies that the complaints function of a national institution should be able to offer something which the legal system or other institutionalized processes cannot. The particular focus of a national institution—human rights—and its ability to develop expertise in this area already offer some concrete advantages to persons who feel that their rights have been violated. The structure and functioning of the complaints mechanism should be such as to allow the national institution to guarantee accessible, rapid and inexpensive resolution of a matter.

221. Whatever the style of the complaints mechanism established by the institution, it is essential that procedural aspects be clearly defined, legally entrenched and rigorously adhered to. Consequently, it will always be preferable that the scope of the institution's powers be founded in law and that its responsibilities towards complainants be precisely defined. The success of any complaints procedure will depend, to a great extent, on the external credibility of the institution. Potential complainants are usually persons who have suffered at he hands of private parties, government officials or administrative bodies. By its actions, a national institution must be in a position to reassure complainants that their grievances will be seriously received and acted on.

2. *Establishing a complaints mechanism*

(a) *What complaints should be investigated?*

222. It is essential that the criteria for admissibility of complaints be clearly established. The first matter to settle is the kind of complaints which will be accepted for investigation. This requires a determination of both the object and the subject-matter of admissible complaints.

223. The object of an admissible complaint is the entity or group of entities against which it can be made. Many offices of the ombudsman, for example, in accordance with their basic objective of ensuring legality and fairness in public administration, restrict the range of possible objects to government departments, government instrumentalities and public officials. A complaint will be considered only if it concerns an action of government. By contrast, a number of other national institutions are empowered to receive and investigate not only complaints against government, but also complaints of human rights violations occurring in other spheres of public life, for example in employment or housing. In these cases, the entity complained against could be an individual, a public or private company, or an organization.

224. The issue of whether a national institution with power to investigate human rights violations should concern itself with acts committed by revolutionary forces and armed opposition groups is a difficult one. Some argue that acts of violence by such groups are clear violations of human rights and, for that reason, must not be

excluded from the institution's mandate. On the other hand, consideration should be given to the fact that, by definition, insurgent groups operate outside national law. For that reason, allegations made against such groups or against individuals associated with them are unlikely to be openly challenged or refuted. Accordingly, it would be virtually impossible for a national institution to conduct an impartial investigation. Ultimately, the matter must be considered within the social and political context of each country, keeping in mind the purposes for which the institution was established; the priorities which it should be encouraged to set; and the fact that acts of violence, whether committed by organized groups or by individuals, are within the jurisdiction of the criminal justice system.

225. A complaints mechanism should clearly define the subject-matter of admissible complaints, i.e. the type of action which can be the basis for complaint. In some cases, the subject-matter will be directly related to the range of permissible objects. An ombudsman-type institution, for example, will generally be restricted to examining allegations of unfairness or illegality in the administrative process.

226. The criteria of admissibility for other institutions may be more directly related to the subject (human rights violation) than the object of a complaint. A national institution may, for example, be generally empowered to investigate violations of civil and political rights, irrespective of who is alleged to have committed the violation.

227. Many provisions establishing the subject-matter of admissible complaints refer to the human rights guarantees contained in constitutions or domestic legislation. The subject-matter of admissible complaints may also be established by specifically setting out the rights to be protected, or the international instruments containing protected rights, violation of which may give rise to an investigation. An institution may, for example, be empowered to investigate violations of human rights defined as all rights guaranteed by the Constitution or embodied in international human rights instruments to which the State in question is a party.

228. In all cases, the subject-matter of admissible complaints should be specified as precisely as possible, avoiding a vaguely worded mandate or a mandate subject to excessively broad interpretation. The power to investigate "human rights violations", for example, would not usefully be interpreted to encompass matters which could properly be handled by other structures, such as breach of contract, defamation or crimes arising out of purely private disputes. Even with a strictly defined mandate, a national institution will almost always be required to establish priorities regarding issues to be considered. While human rights elements may be found in almost every area of human activity, an effective national institution must interpret its subject-matter mandate in a way which avoids misallocation of human and financial resources. An effective national institution will also ensure that nothing in this regard negatively affects external perceptions of its competence, thereby discouraging the submission of genuine grievances.

(b) *Are restrictions appropriate?*

229. Many national institutions impose restrictions on both the object and subject-matter of complaints. The issue of restrictions is a delicate one and it must be recalled that each State has the right to establish the type of institution best suited to its own cultural and legal traditions. At the same time, it is essential that restrictions do not prevent the institution from fulfilling the purposes for which it was established.

230. Restrictions on the object of a complaint are common. For example, a national institution will not generally be granted the power to deal with complaints against members of the legislature or the judiciary. Other restrictions may relate to the institution's specific functions. For example, an institution established to oversee fairness and legality in public administration will naturally be precluded from acting on complaints of violations committed by private entities or individuals.

231. Most national institutions will not be permitted to consider issues which are already the subject of scrutiny by another body. Electoral complaints, for example, could be specifically excluded from the field of competence of a particular institution if the granting of such power would conflict with the mandate of another agency. Such restrictions are also important where there is a possibility of a conflict of jurisdiction between the institution and another body, for example where a particular matter is already under judicial consideration (see paras. 91 ff. above).

232. Other restrictions on the object of a complaint may be more problematic. It is clear, for example, that preventing a national institution from investigating violations committed by the police severely reduces the institution's potential effectiveness as a protector of human rights. Designating the military as exempt from the complaints mechanism may also have a detrimental effect on an institution's effectiveness, particularly in view of the strength of the military in many States and its corresponding potential to violate human rights. While respecting differences between national institutions, it may be said that an "inappropriate" restriction on the object of a complaint will be one which prevents or restricts the capacity of the institution to perform the functions or discharge the responsibilities with which it has been entrusted.

233. As already mentioned (para. 227 above), complaints must generally relate to constitutionally conferred rights or rights embodied in legislative provisions or otherwise recognized as part of national law. Restrictions on the subject-matter of a complaint will generally reflect this requirement as well as the specific responsibilities with which the institution has been entrusted. A commission against racial discrimination, for example, will, by virtue of its specific mandate, be prevented from conducting examinations of other forms of discrimination, except in so far as these can be related to its principal focus.

234. A number of national institutions are empowered to investigate only complaints of violations of civil and political rights. While this may be a means of ensuring an appropriate workload for the institution, it is im-

portant to recognize that all human rights have equivalent and indivisible status in international law and that violations of economic, social and cultural rights are equally capable of documentation and investigation.

(c) *Who may complain?*

235. Most of the complaints mechanisms of national institutions specifically provide that any person is entitled to lodge a complaint against the objects over which the institution is granted jurisdiction. In some legislative provisions the term "any person" is defined to include non-citizens and refugees. Legislation may also proclaim the right of children and prisoners to make a complaint.

236. The question whether "any person" includes an association of persons should be directly addressed in the legislation establishing the complaints procedure. Some national institutions have taken the position that, if the alleged violation of rights affected an organization as an identifiable entity and not just one of its members, then the organization has standing to complain. Specificity in legislation is desirable as detailed provisions can prevent technical arguments over standing to complain.

(i) Complaints by third parties

237. It is generally accepted that, in principle, a complaint should be lodged by the person against whom the alleged violation(s) occurred. There are good reasons for such a requirement. It is the alleged victim who has the best knowledge of the incident and who should properly have the freedom to decide whether or not to make a complaint.

238. Nevertheless, it is sometimes the case that those most vulnerable to human rights violations are not in a position to invoke protective mechanisms such as a complaints procedure. There are many reasons why it may be impossible for a complaint to be lodged by the person who has suffered the violation. It may be that that person is a child or is disabled by physical or mental incapacity. In other situations, the victim of a human rights violation may have disappeared, be held in custody incommunicado, or be dead. Because of these very real possibilities, it is essential that formal provision be made for representative complaints which may be lodged by a relative, friend, legal representative or concerned non-governmental organization on behalf of an alleged victim.

(ii) Class actions

239. A number of national institutions have developed a procedure for receiving class actions, whereby an individual affected by a human rights violation is able to complain not only on his or her own behalf, but also on behalf of others who are similarly affected.

240. This possibility of representative complaints helps to ensure that widespread problems are treated as such and are not approached as isolated aberrations. In addition, regardless of how thorough the investigative process has been and how appropriate the remedies are, resolution of an individual complaint may not always be enough to secure the necessary changes within government or wider society.

241. Where class actions are possible, strict guidelines are usually established to determine the suitability of an issue or complaint for this kind of resolution. A national institution may, for example, require some or all of the following conditions to be fulfilled before a complaint is accepted as a class action:

The complainant must be a member of the class affected or likely to be affected;

The complainant must personally have been affected by the alleged violation;

The class of persons affected or potentially affected is so numerous that it is impossible to deal with the matter simply by joining a number of specified individuals to the complaint;

There are questions of law or fact common to the members of the class, and the claims of the complainant are typical of the claims of the class;

Multiple complaints would be likely to produce inconsistent results;

The grounds for action appear to apply to the whole class, making it appropriate to grant remedies to the class as a whole.

(d) *Procedure for submitting complaints*

242. A complaint is usually submitted by way of written statement, although there should be capacity to receive and act on an oral complaint, if necessary. The lodging of a complaint should be free of charge and efforts should be made to ensure that, as far as possible, complainants incur no direct or indirect costs. In this context, it may be useful to consider establishing contact points throughout the country, particularly in remote areas, to accept and assist in the preparation of complaints. It will always be preferable for a complaint to be lodged directly with the institution: use of intermediaries, such as government bodies or members of parliament, will invariably delay and complicate the process.

243. National institutions should ensure the availability of information materials in appropriate languages, which set out the procedure for lodging complaints in clear terms. The provision of such information will eliminate any need for a complaint to be lodged in person. To require personal attendance at the office of the national institution would disadvantage complainants living in remote areas and those without ready transportation.

244. Consideration should be given to implementing procedures which encourage and facilitate the lodging of complaints. The social and ethnic profile of a community may require, for example, provision of interpreters or trained assistants. The possibility of electronic communication of complaints may, in other circumstances, be an important factor in expediting the process. An independent analysis of the constituency of each institution is necessary in order to determine the ways in which submission of complaints can be made easier.

245. It is important to note that excessively formal procedures for submitting complaints may discourage victims from seeking help from the institution and result in unacceptable delays in initiating investigations. In the same way, procedures which are inappropriate to the cul-

tural traditions and economic status of those whose rights are most likely to be violated will not facilitate the complaints process. A requirement that allegations be confirmed by affidavit, for example, may be inappropriate and unnecessarily onerous in situations where vulnerable groups are poor, live in remote areas and have neither the physical means nor the necessary legal literacy. Formalism and unnecessary bureaucratic procedure can cause irreparable damage to an institution's public image, as well as to its efficiency. For these reasons, national institutions should make every effort to ensure that procedures for submitting complaints are as simple as possible.

(e) *Issues of confidentiality*

246. It is a usual requirement that written complaints be signed by the victim or by the person lodging the complaint on his or her behalf. There are logical reasons for not permitting anonymous complaints, including the fact that national institutions have no way of verifying the validity of an anonymous complaint and cannot provide redress to an unknown victim. However, the fact that complaints cannot be made anonymously requires steps to be taken to ensure confidentiality.

247. In the case of all complaints, and particularly in circumstances involving allegations of human rights violations by public officials, victims must be left in no doubt that their decision to come forward does not compromise their safety in any way. To be in a position to offer such a guarantee, a national institution must develop confidentiality structures and procedures— beginning with receipt of the complaint and continuing, as far as possible, throughout the investigatory process. Confidentiality should not, of course, be imposed on complainants against their wishes.

(f) *Rejecting a complaint*

248. All preconditions regarding the object and subject-matter of a complaint must be met before the complaint can be formally accepted. If a condition in this regard is not met, a national institution is entitled to reject the complaint on the grounds that it does not fall within the institution's jurisdiction.

249. Other grounds for rejection of a complaint at the preliminary stage are common. National institutions are generally entitled to reject a complaint which, even without further investigation, is clearly frivolous, unwarranted or unfounded in law. Rejection may also occur when it is decided that the connection between the complaint and the complainant is not sufficiently direct. This latter situation is generally referred to as a question of standing. If a time-limit has been established (between commission of the act complained of and lodgement of the complaint), a complaint made outside that time-limit may legitimately be rejected.

250. In all situations where a complaint is rejected, it is essential that the institution inform the complainant of the precise reasons for the rejection. Where appropriate, the institution should also inform the complainant of the existence of any alternative procedures which may be available. National institutions should always ensure that the party who filed the petition is informed of his or her rights and that he or she has access to all available remedies. Any delay in formulating or communicating a decision to reject a complaint should be avoided. Quick action at this preliminary stage will ensure that the complainant is able to take full advantage of alternative means of redress. It will also enhance the public image of the institution as a competent and helpful body.

3. *Conciliating a complaint*

251. As already noted, national human rights institutions are an alternative dispute-resolution mechanism. There are three general variants of dispute resolution: arbitration, in which a third party such as a national institution can make binding decisions; conciliation, in which the third party makes strongly weighted although non-binding recommendations; and mediation, where the third party controls the process without having any influence on the content and, again, without issuing a decision. National institutions are especially involved in the two latter procedures.

252. Many national institutions are directed to encourage the settlement of complaints by conciliation instead of, or before, launching their own investigation into the matter. Conciliation will involve bringing the two parties together in an effort to ascertain the facts of the case and to effect a mutually acceptable resolution. The advantages of such an approach have been amply demonstrated at the international level, particularly by the International Labour Organisation, which now emphasizes the practice of conciliation in its own work, as well as in the instruments which it adopts.

253. At the national level, conciliation of complaints regarding violations of human rights, particularly with regard to allegations of discrimination, has proved very successful. Conciliation obviates the need for a formal investigation, which can be both expensive and time-consuming. It is also less confrontational in procedure and effect and, for this reason, is particularly valuable in situations where securing a change in attitude or behaviour is considered more important than punishing a violation.

254. The cooperation of both parties is essential for conciliation to be a useful means of dispute settlement. For that reason, the ultimate success of the procedure will often depend on the existence of other recourse mechanisms which may be invoked if the conciliation process is a failure.

255. It should be noted that, in the same way that an investigation of the facts of a case will benefit from the expertise of trained personnel, effective conciliation requires the participation of skilled conciliators. The question of training in these and other areas has already been discussed (paras. 126 ff. above). The task of conciliation can also be eased by the drafting of guidelines which are made available to the parties as well as to the conciliator. The application of guidelines to particular cases may also result in the development of useful precedent, for consideration in subsequent, similar cases.

4. *Conducting an investigation*

256. Once a complaint has been formally accepted (i.e. when all the conditions for admissibility have been met), the national institution may begin an investigation

of the complaint on its merits. The aim of the investigation is to ascertain whether a violation or illegality (as defined by the mandate of the institution) has occurred and, if so, which person or agency is responsible.

(a) *Powers of investigation*

257. In most situations, the investigation of a complaint will be carried out by the national institution or by persons acting under its direct authority and control. To conduct an effective investigation, the institution must have certain resources at its disposal, including trained staff and sufficient financial means.

258. In the same way, the granting of certain basic powers to an institution is essential in order to permit efficient investigations. There are no universally appropriate rules in this regard, and the powers with which a national institution is vested will vary according to the nature of its complaints machinery and the functions which it was established to fulfil. In all circumstances, however, the institution must be granted the legal capacity to discover whether the complaint is founded and, if so, who is responsible. Without this capacity, the complaints mechanism will be useless.

259. Both investigative and adjudicative powers are fundamental to conducting an efficient and effective investigation of an alleged human rights violation. These powers may include the following:

Power to inform the object of the complaint of the allegations made, in order to permit that person or body to reply to such allegations;

Free access to all documents, including public records, which, in the opinion of the investigating body, are necessary for proper investigation of the complaint;

Power to compel the production of relevant information (either in the form of documents or by means of oral evidence);

Freedom to conduct on-site investigations if necessary, including visitorial powers over jails, detention facilities, etc.;

Power to call parties to a hearing;

Power to grant immunity from prosecution to persons giving testimony or otherwise appearing as witnesses;

Power to hear and question every individual (including experts and representatives of government agencies and, if appropriate, private entities) who, in the opinion of the investigating body, has knowledge concerning the alleged violation or is otherwise in a position to assist the investigation;

For the latter purpose, power to summon witnesses and compel their appearance; to receive oral and written evidence under oath; and to compel the production of such documents or other material evidence from public agencies and authorities as the investigating body considers necessary for proper investigation of the complaint.

260. The investigatory powers of a number of national institutions are supplemented by a general clause granting the institution the power to engage in all other (unspecified) activities which, in its opinion, are necessary for conducting a proper investigation. Such an umbrella clause will permit a certain flexibility in the investigatory procedure which may be highly desirable. It is, however, important for an institution granted discretionary powers to remain aware of its own obligations to respect the human rights of all persons at every stage of the investigation.

(b) *Investigatory procedures*

261. The granting of sufficient and appropriate powers is not, in itself, enough to ensure the conduct of a proper investigation. A national institution must also develop its own standards and guidelines (including rules of procedure) to be applied to all investigations.

262. While each institution must formulate its own procedures in this regard, a few general comments here my be useful. First, guidelines should reflect the responsibilities which the institution has been given and the powers which it has been granted to discharge those responsibilities. Secondly, while providing the necessary operational flexibility, they should also establish a fixed procedure which is not deviated from except in certain clearly defined circumstances. Thirdly, they should set measurable goals of efficiency and timeliness.

263. Specific issues which should be addressed in connection with the investigatory process include the standard of proof to be adopted. The investigatory body can rightly be considered the best judge of evidentiary matters, and therefore may be permitted a certain degree of flexibility in this regard. In situations where a matter is not covered by legislation, consideration should be given to the adoption of a civil "balance of probabilities" standards rather than the criminal-law standard of "beyond reasonable doubt". The adoption of the former type of standard may be justified in view of the evidentiary problems which can exist in many situations of suspected human rights violations and the fact that the objective of most investigatory mechanisms is remedial rather than punitive.

264. The ability of a national institution to call upon expert assistance may be crucial to the efficient performance of its investigatory tasks. Some institutions are able to choose government officials and members of the police or other forces who are, in the institution's opinion, best suited to the task at hand. Where such a possibility exists, it is essential that provision be made to ensure that experts seconded from government forces or offices are able to work independently of their parent unit. In this regard, it is important to avoid a situation where expert assistance is recruited from the same branch or area of government as the individual or agency under investigation.

265. Investigatory procedure should include provision for specific legal protection from retaliation for individuals who have filed a complaint or participated in the investigation of a complaint. The nature of many human rights violations renders it likely that victim or witnesses will fear reprisals for their decision to come forward. The national institution should be able to adopt its own procedures for protection of witnesses and sufficient resources should be allocated for that purpose.

266. A number of national institutions have recognized the importance of a power to impose sanctions on individuals and agencies who obstruct or fail to cooper-

ate in an investigation. At the very least, a national institution should be empowered to refer the matter to another body for consideration or action where it is of the opinion that its investigation cannot be properly conducted because of obstruction or failure to cooperate.

267. It is important that guidelines and standards for investigating complaints be made public. This will serve to inform complainants of the investigatory process in which they are involved and is also likely to enhance public confidence in the institution as a competent body for receiving and acting on allegations of human rights violations. The same advantages may be derived from holding all hearings in public and permitting public scrutiny of the investigatory process. Private or closed hearings should be held only in exceptional cases and then only following a public statement of the reasons why a particular hearing must be held in camera.

5. *Remedies for violations*

268. The powers of national institutions to take action or provide remedies following conclusion of an investigation (or failure to conciliate a dispute) vary widely. Some institutions have been granted considerable authority in terms of imposing penalties or referring a matter to a higher body. Other institutions must restrict their follow-up activities to recommendations which are transmitted to parliament or to the appropriate government agency for further action.

269. As with the investigatory process itself, there are no universally applicable rules on the subject of remedies. What is appropriate for a particular institution will depend on the structure of its complaints mechanism and the particular goals which it was established to fulfil. However, while recognizing inevitable differences, its is also important to acknowledge that powers to receive and investigate violations are of little utility without a corresponding ability to provide remedies for violations. The lack of such ability, as well as operating to discourage the submission of complaints, is likely to undermine the credibility of the complaints procedure itself.

270. The powers which may be granted to a national institution to facilitate follow-up of complaints and remedial action in the case of violations are discussed below.

(a) *Power to recommend*

271. In almost all situations, a national institution will be empowered to submit recommendations concerning matters which it has been conciliating or investigating. Depending on the jurisdiction of the institution, a recommendation may be addressed to a government agency, a public official, a private individual or an organization. It may propose the adoption of measures to prevent or lessen the effects of a human rights violation; it may suggest a change in practice or procedure or a reconsideration or reversal of a decision; or it may advocate an apology or payment of damages, or advise on alternative remedial action. Recommendations may concern one particular case or be made within a broader context of attempting to prevent a reoccurrence of detrimental activity or behaviour.

272. Irrespective of its object or subject-matter, a recommendation, by definition, will never be binding; its acceptance by any party must be voluntary and cannot be forced. In certain situations, however, failure to take account of recommendations made in respect of a complaint may entitle the national institution to refer the matter to another body for consideration (see paras. 273 ff. below).

(b) *Powers of referral*

273. A national institution may be empowered to refer a case which it has investigated or attempted to conciliate to another responsible agency. Referral could be made to the relevant ministry, to another government agency or a tribunal established for that purpose, to parliament, to the judiciary, or to prosecuting authorities.

274. Powers of referral will generally be invoked as a second or subsequent step in the process of resolving a complaint. A national institution may, for example, be entitled to refer a complaint if:

The entity in respect of which a recommendation has been made, or against which a decision has been taken, does not take account of the recommendation or refuses to comply with the decision within a specified time-limit;

A settlement of the case cannot be secured;

The terms of an agreed settlement have not been met;

The national institution is of the opinion that its own investigation cannot be properly conducted because of obstructions or failure to obtain necessary cooperation;

The investigation gives rise to reasonable suspicion that a criminal act or disciplinary offence under law has been committed which warrants intervention by prosecuting authorities;

The investigation reveals that the matter may be more appropriately dealt with by another body or agency.

275. Referral may also be appropriate where one or both parties are dissatisfied with the results of an investigation or with a decision taken by the national institution in regard to a complaint. Any avenues of review or appeal which are available should be specifically set out in the law or guidelines under which the institution operates and be communicated to all parties affected by a decision of the institution.

276. The responsibilities of a national institution with respect to a particular case will not necessarily end when the matter has been referred elsewhere. If the matter has been referred to a court or tribunal, for example, the national institution should be able to appear before such a body in support of the complainant's case. In all situations, however, guidelines and procedures for following up referred complaints should be elaborated in order to ensure that the complaints are dealt with fully and appropriately.

(c) *Power to make determinations*

277. A national institution may be granted a variety of specific powers beyond recommendation and referral with the aim of providing relief to victims of human rights violations. The type of relief awarded is largely dependent on the nature of the violation. In cases where

the violation can be neutralized or its effects lessened, the national institution may order the reversal of a particular administrative decision or a change in practice or policy. Where the situation cannot be restored to that which existed prior to the violation, methods of redress may include the ordering of a public apology or the award of damages or compensation.

278. The ability of a national institution to order interim injunctions or interim relief during the course of an investigation can be extremely valuable. Such interim measures are generally directed towards ensuring that the position of the complainant is not made worse during the investigation or conciliation process, or that this process is not obstructed by subsequent events.

(d) *Power to make enforceable orders*

279. A national institution may be granted the power to make legally enforceable orders and binding decisions. Such power will generally permit the institution to seize a higher body (e.g. a tribunal, court or prosecutor's office) in the event that a party refuses to comply with a decision within a given time. Even if the actual enforcement procedure is entrusted to another body, the power to make enforceable orders will benefit the national institution by considerably strengthening its authority with regard to complaints of human rights violations.

(e) *Publishing decisions*

280. In addition to other specific capacities to effect redress, national institutions will generally be empowered to publish the results of an investigation or conciliation, along with any recommendations made or decisions taken in that regard. This is not, strictly speaking, a remedial power, and competence in this respect should generally co-exist with other mechanisms for remedy and redress. Nevertheless, the ability to make public its findings is an essential prerequisite for establishing the credibility of a complaints mechanism and ensuring maximum effectiveness within the limits of its prescribed powers.

281. Publication also serves several other identifiable purposes, not least of which is to inform public opinion and provoke discussion. This can be particularly important in situations where the basis of the subject complaint exists within wider problems of discrimination or unfairness which may subsequently need to be addressed by parliament or another branch of government. Publication of the results of an investigation can also be an effective means of assuring both present and future complainants that such matters are taken seriously by the institution.

282. As far as possible, publication of investigation results and decisions should take into consideration the confidentiality needs of the parties. It may not always be necessary, for example, to publicize details of the complainants.

C. Investigations or public inquiries *suo moto*

283. National institutions may have jurisdiction to initiate investigations or inquiries into possible situations of human rights violations without the need to receive a

formal complaint or invitation from a government agency.

284. The power to conduct investigations *suo moto* can be an extremely important and far-reaching one. Children, women, the poor, the homeless, the mentally or physically incapacitated, prisoners, and members of religious, ethnic and linguistic minorities are all, due to their unequal status, especially vulnerable to human rights abuses. It is ironic but generally true that these same vulnerable groups are also most likely to be unaware of their rights and of the mechanisms which exist to protect those rights. Even where knowledge does exist, victims of human rights violations do not often have advocates to act on their behalf and may be extremely reluctant to approach an official agency in order to lodge a formal complaint.

285. It is occasionally said that, since ministries and government departments are legally and administratively capable of conducting inquiries, there is little need to duplicate this function by granting to national institutions the right to launch their own investigations. This assertion must be answered by referring to the fact that, in almost every part of the world, national and international human rights standards have not yet been sufficiently integrated into the administrative infrastructure or into the consciousness of government officials. For example, an inquiry into housing conducted without reference to human rights principles may look at homelessness purely as a problem in the supply of housing. A human rights approach will consider, *inter alia*, the issue of accessibility to adequate housing as well as the rights of particular groups to special protection. An inquiry into mental illness conducted with reference to human rights will go beyond an analysis of legal protection to consider a much wider range of rights, including entitlement to treatment, rehabilitation, education, counselling, economic and social security, and protection from discrimination.

286. A national institution with the capacity to initiate its own investigations may be able to make a significant contribution to ensuring that vulnerable groups are given a public voice and that human rights violations, wherever they occur, become a matter of general knowledge and concern.

1. *Selecting the issue for investigation*

287. In some circumstances, an effective complaints procedure can operate as a barometer of the current social situation with respect to human rights, at least in so far as the mandate of the national institution is concerned. Complaints procedures which exist within the international human rights system have been performing this indicative function for many years. Communications received under a particular instrument or in relation to a particular issue are scrutinized in an effort to isolate particularly acute problems and identify negative trends. Where such problems or trends emerge, the body concerned may use this information as a basis for launching an investigation.

288. National institutions vested with competence to receive individual complaints and to initiate their own inquiries can usefully follow this practice by screening

all complaints received in order to determine the existence of any trend or pattern which may indicate the need for further investigation.

289. However, for the reasons already stated (paras. 284-285 above), a complaints mechanism will not always accurately reflect the current human rights situation. A national institution must therefore ensure that it establishes alternative procedures by which to identify existing and potential problems. Such procedures will include developing and strengthening relationships with community and non-governmental organizations, which, because of their functions, are likely to be aware of difficulties and problems existing within society. A national institution can also conduct its day-to-day affairs in such a way as to ensure maximum contact with its constituency. The media may be another useful focal point for indentifying cases of maladministration, illegalities and human rights violations committed by both government and private entities.

2. *Conducting an investigation* suo moto

290. As regards both necessary powers and desirable procedures, there will be little distinction between an investigation of an individual complaint and a more general inquiry into a particular issue or situation. In addition to obvious dissimilarities in scope, differences will generally relate to the objective of the investigation or inquiry.

291. As already indicated, the aim of an investigation into an individual complaint will be to ascertain whether a violation or illegality has occurred and, if so, which person or agency is responsible. While a general inquiry can have similar aims, it will also be concerned with the wider implications of the issue or situation. This wider concern will require the investigators to address more difficult and far-reaching questions, including how such violations came about; what practices, arrangements or policies contributed to them; and what measures should be taken to ensure that the situation improves or the violations do not reoccur. Rarely will such questions be satisfactorily addressed by providing redress to individual victims. Instead, a national institution may find it necessary to address a range of political, social and economic variables in an effort to ascertain the cause and thereby make useful suggestions as to the cure.

292. If an inquiry is designated as "public", a national institution should take concrete steps to ensure that background documents and other information are made available for general scrutiny and that all hearings are conducted openly. Efforts should be made to publicize the inquiry in a way which ensures that ready access is available to persons in possession of information or in a position to hold an opinion on the subject under consideration.

3. *Follow-up*

293. The question of follow-up will usually relate to the specific powers which have been granted to a national institution with regard to self-initiated investigations. As with individual complaints, the institution is likely to be empowered to transmit recommendations, based on its findings, to the relevant government department or agency. It may also be able to use other powers to lobby parliament for legislative reforms (see paras. 190 ff. above).

294. Regardless of its specific powers of follow-up, a national institution should make every effort to ensure that the results of its inquiries are made public and disseminated as widely as possible. Measures taken with respect to recommendations made should be carefully monitored and an account of action by government agencies or the legislature in response to such recommendations should be incorporated into the annual report of the institution.

D. Intervening in legal proceedings

295. A national institution may be granted the power to intervene in legal proceedings (usually by submitting *amicus curiae* briefs) in cases brought under human rights legislation or which otherwise involve human rights issues over which the institution has competence. The institution can use this opportunity to ensure that the court is made aware of the human rights implications of the case at hand and of the relevant national and international standards.

296. The capacity to intervene in judicial proceedings is not automatic and leave of the court to intervene must be sought. The granting of such leave will generally be conditional on the institution demonstrating an interest in the matter at hand. This should not be difficult if the case is brought under domestic human rights legislation. In other situations, the national institution may need to show that human rights considerations are involved and, in the absence of a directly applicable legislative provision, that there is a basis in domestic law for the application of international human rights standards.

297. A national institution may also be able to appear in court to support orders for the enforcement of its determinations.

CONCLUSION

298. There are some who see no good reason for establishing special machinery devoted to the promotion and protection of human rights. They may argue that such bodies are not a wise use of scarce resources and that an independent judiciary and democratically elected parliament are sufficient to ensure that human rights abuses do not occur.

299. Unfortunately, history has taught us differently. An institution which is in some way separated from the responsibilities of executive governance and judicial administration is in a position to take a leading role in the field of human rights. By maintaining its real and perceived distance from the Government of the day,

such a body can make a unique contribution to a country's efforts to protect its citizens and to develop a culture respectful of human rights and fundamental freedoms.

300. This handbook has attempted to identify the main elements which can contribute to the effective functioning of national human rights institutions in their efforts to enhance public awareness, educate about human rights, advise and assist government on legislation and policy, and investigate alleged human rights violations. The handbook is the result of expertise developed both within and outside the United Nations Centre for Human Rights and will provide a framework for the further development of the Centre's programme in this area.

ANNEXES

Annex I

PRINCIPLES RELATING TO THE STATUS OF NATIONAL INSTITUTIONS[a]

Competence and responsibilities

1. A national institution shall be vested with competence to promote and protect human rights.

2. A national institution shall be given as broad a mandate as possible, which shall be clearly set forth in a constitutional or legislative text, specifying its composition and its sphere of competence.

3. A national institution shall, *inter alia*, have the following responsibilities:

(a) To submit to the Government, Parliament and any other competent body, on an advisory basis either at the request of the authorities concerned or through the exercise of its power to hear a matter without higher referral, opinions, recommendations, proposals and reports on any matters concerning the promotion and protection of human rights; the national institution may decide to publicize them; these opinions, recommendations, proposals and reports, as well as any prerogative of the national institution, shall relate to the following areas:

(i) Any legislative or administrative provisions, as well as provisions relating to judicial organization, intended to preserve and extend the protection of human rights; in that connection, the national institution shall examine the legislation and administrative provisions in force, as well as bills and proposals, and shall make such recommendations as it deems appropriate in order to ensure that these provisions conform to the fundamental principles of human rights; it shall, if necessary, recommend the adoption of new legislation, the amendment of legislation in force and the adoption or amendment of administrative measures;

(ii) Any situation of violation of human rights which it decides to take up;

(iii) The preparation of reports on the national situation with regard to human rights in general, and on more specific matters;

(iv) Drawing the attention of the Government to situations in any part of the country where human rights are violated and making proposals to it for initiatives to put an end to such situations and, where necessary, expressing an opinion on the positions and reactions of the Government;

(b) To promote and ensure the harmonization of national legislation, regulations and practices with the international human rights instruments to which the State is a party, and their effective implementation;

(c) To encourage ratification of the above-mentioned instruments or accession to those instruments, and to ensure their implementation;

(d) To contribute to the reports which States are required to submit to United Nations bodies and committees, and to regional institutions, pursuant to their treaty obligations, and, where necessary, to express an opinion on the subject, with due respect for their independence;

(e) To cooperate with the United Nations and any other organization in the United Nations system, the regional institutions and the national institutions of other countries that are competent in the areas of the promotion and protection of human rights;

(f) To assist in the formulation of programmes for the teaching of, and research into, human rights and to take part in their execution in schools, universities and professional circles;

(g) To publicize human rights and efforts to combat all forms of discrimination, in particular racial discrimination, by increasing public awareness; especially through information and education and by making use of all press organs.

Composition and guarantees of independence and pluralism

1. The composition of the national institution and the appointment of its members; whether by means of an election or otherwise, shall be established in accordance with a procedure which affords all necessary guarantees to ensure the pluralist representation of the social forces (of civilian society) involved in the promotion and protection of human rights, particularly by powers which will enable effective cooperation to be established with, or through the presence of, representatives of:

(a) Non-governmental organizations responsible for human rights and efforts to combat racial discrimination, trade unions, concerned social and professional organizations, for example, associations of lawyers, doctors, journalists and eminent scientists;

(b) Trends in philosophical or religious thought;

(c) Universities and qualified experts;

(d) Parliament;

(e) Government departments (if they are included, these representatives should participate in the deliberations only in an advisory capacity).

2. The national institution shall have an infrastructure which is suited to the smooth conduct of its activities, in particular adequate funding. The purpose of this funding should be to enable it to have its own staff and premises, in order to be independent of the Government and not be subject to financial control which might affect its independence.

3. In order to ensure a stable mandate for the members of the institution, without which there can be no real independence, their appointment shall be effected by an official act which shall establish the specific duration of the mandate. This mandate may be renewable, provided that the pluralism of the institution's membership is ensured.

Methods of operation

Within the framework of its operation, the national institution shall:

(a) Freely consider any questions falling within its competence, whether they are submitted by the Government or taken up by it without referral to a higher authority, on the proposal of its members or of any petitioner;

(b) Hear any person and obtain any information and any documents necessary for assessing situations falling within its competence;

(c) Address public opinion directly or through any press organ, particularly in order to publicize its opinions and recommendations;

(d) Meet on a regular basis and whenever necessary in the presence of all its members after they have been duly convened;

(e) Establish working groups from among its members as necessary, and set up local or regional sections to assist it in discharging its functions;

---

[a] Commission on Human Rights resolution 1992/54 of 3 March 1992, annex (*Official Records of the Economic and Social Council, 1992, Supplement No. 2* (E/1992/22), chap. II, sect. A); General Assembly resolution 48/134 of 20 December 1993, annex.

(*f*) Maintain consultation with the other bodies, whether jurisdictional or otherwise, responsible for the promotion and protection of human rights (in particular, ombudsmen, mediators and similar institutions);

(*g*) In view of the fundamental role played by non-governmental organizations in expanding the work of national institutions, develop relations with non-governmental organizations devoted to promoting and protecting human rights, to economic and social development, to combating racism, to protecting particularly vulnerable groups (especially children, migrant workers, refugees, physically and mentally disabled persons) or to specialized areas.

Additional principles concerning the status of commissions with quasi-jurisdictional competence

A national institution may be authorized to hear and consider complaints and petitions concerning individual situations. Cases may be brought before it by individuals, their representatives, third parties, non-governmental organizations, associations of trade unions or any other representative organizations. In such circumstances, and without prejudice to the principles stated above concerning the other powers of the commissions, the functions entrusted to them may be based on the following principles:

(*a*) Seeking an amicable settlement through conciliation or, within the limits prescribed by the law, through binding decisions or, where necessary, on the basis of confidentiality;

(*b*) Informing the party who filed the petition of his rights, in particular the remedies available to him, and promoting his access to them;

(*c*) Hearing any complaints or petitions or transmitting them to any other competent authority within the limits prescribed by the law;

(*d*) Making recommendations to the competent authorities, especially by proposing amendments or reforms of the laws, regulations and administrative practices, especially if they have created the difficulties encountered by the persons filing the petitions in order to assert their rights.

Annex II

CONTACTS AND RESOURCE POINTS

African Centre for Democraty and Human Rights Studies
Kairabi Avenue
Banjul   Tel.: (220) 394525/394961
THE GAMBIA   Fax: (220) 394962

Centre for Human Rights
United Nations
8-14, avenue de la Paix
1211 Geneva 10   Tel.: (4122) 907 1234
SWITZERLAND   Fax: (4122) 917 0123

Commonwealth Secretariat
Human Rights Unit
Marlborough House
Pall Mall
London SW1Y 5HX   Tel.: (4471) 839 3411
UNITED KINGDOM   Fax: (4171) 930 0827

Human Rights Information Centre
Council of Europe
67075 Strasbourg   Tel.: (3388) 41 28 18
FRANCE   Fax: (3388) 41 27 04

Inter-American Institute of Human Rights
Apartado postal 10-081
1000 San José   Tel.: (506) 234 0404
COSTA RICA   Fax: (506) 234 0955

International Ombudsman Institute
Room 205-D, Weir Library
Law Centre
University of Alberta
Edmonton T6 G2 H5   Tel.: (1403) 492 3196
CANADA   Fax: (1403) 492 4924

Annex III

INFORMATION NOTE ON THE TECHNICAL COOPERATION PROGRAMME OF THE UNITED NATIONS CENTRE FOR HUMAN RIGHTS AS IT RELATES TO NATIONAL INSTITUTIONS

1. The technical cooperation programme of the Centre for Human Rights is one means by which the United Nations seeks to achieve the objective set forth in its Charter of promoting respect for human rights and for fundamental freedoms. The principal goal of the programme is to promote the meaningful application of international human rights norms at the national level. Assistance is provided following requests from Member States and a careful assessment of needs is generally carried out prior to the development and implementation of a concrete proposal. Programme elements include constitutional and legislative reform assistance; training in the administration of justice (for judges, lawyers, prosecutors, police, military and prison personnel); electoral assistance; training of government officials in the preparation of reports to treaty-monitoring bodies; provision of fellowships; and promotional and educational activities.

2. A central focus of the technical cooperation programme is the consolidation and strengthening of the role which national institutions can play in the promotion and protection of human rights. To that end, the Centre for Human Rights has developed an action plan setting out a number of objectives, including assisting in the creation of new institutions and the strengthening of existing institutions, and fostering cooperation between institutions.

3. First, the Centre offers its services to Governments which are considering or in the process of establishing a national human rights institution. It is during this preparatory phase that crucial decisions concerning the nature, functions, powers and responsibilities of the institution will be taken. Assistance at this stage will generally involve provision of the services of experts to advise government authorities on suitable models, from a comparative perspective, as well as to pro-

vide technical information to facilitate the task of legislative drafting. Expert assistance can also be provided to help a new institution in the development of criteria and procedures for the recruitment and selection of key personnel.

4. Technical assistance to established national institutions must, of course, be accommodated within the existing legislative framework. In such cases, the Centre is able to offer a variety of forms of assistance (including training of staff) aimed at strengthening an institution and enhancing its capacity to play an effective role in human rights promotion and protection.

5. The objective of fostering cooperation between institutions is pursued on a number of different fronts. Governments wishing to establish a human rights institution can benefit from the practical experience of others who have already gone through this process. Those involved in the operation of existing institutions can enhance mutual strengthening by exchanging information and experience. Existing institutions can also cooperate on a practical level by conducting joint activities and collaborating in studies or research projects. The Centre for Human Rights facilitates these contacts by providing for exchange fellowships and assisting in the organization of international, regional and subregional activities, including training courses, seminars, workshops and periodic meetings.

6. Requests for technical assistance may be made by any national institution direct to the High Commissioner for Human Rights, United Nations, Palais des Nations, 1211 Geneva 10, Switzerland. Requests for further information may be addressed to the Chief, Technical Cooperation Branch, United Nations Centre for Human Rights, at the same address.

Annex IV

INTERNATIONAL BILL OF HUMAN RIGHTS

1. UNIVERSAL DECLARATION OF HUMAN RIGHTS

Preamble

Whereas recognition of the inherent dignity and of the equal and inalienable rights of all members of the human family is the foundation of freedom, justice and peace in the world,

Whereas disregard and contempt for human rights have resulted in barbarous acts which have outraged the conscience of mankind, and the advent of a world in which human beings shall enjoy freedom of speech and belief and freedom from fear and want has been proclaimed as the highest aspiration of the common people,

Whereas it is essential, if man is not to be compelled to have recourse, as a last resort, to rebellion against tyranny and oppression, that human rights should be protected by the rule of law,

Whereas it is essential to promote the development of friendly relations between nations,

Whereas the peoples of the United Nations have in the Charter reaffirmed their faith in fundamental human rights, in the dignity and worth of the human person and in the equal rights of men and women and have determined to promote social progress and better standards of life in larger freedom,

Whereas Member States have pledged themselves to achieve, in cooperation with the United Nations, the promotion of universal respect for and observance of human rights and fundamental freedoms,

Whereas a common understanding of these rights and freedoms is of the greatest importance for the full realization of this pledge,

Now, therefore,

The General Assembly

Proclaims this Universal Declaration of Human Rights as a common standard of achievement for all peoples and all nations, to the end that every individual and every organ of society, keeping this Declaration constantly in mind, shall strive by teaching and education to promote respect for these rights and freedoms and by progressive measures, national and international, to secure their universal and effective recognition and observance, both among the peoples of Member States themselves and among the peoples of territories under their jurisdiction.

Article 1

All human beings are born free and equal in dignity and rights. They are endowed with reason and conscience and should act towards one another in a spirit of brotherhood.

Article 2

Everyone is entitled to all the rights and freedoms set forth in this Declaration, without distinction of any kind, such as race, colour, sex, language, religion, political or other opinion, national or social origin, property, birth or other status.

Furthermore, no distinction shall be made on the basis of the political, jurisdictional or international status of the country or territory to which a person belongs, whether it be independent, trust, non-self-governing or under any other limitation of sovereignty.

Article 3

Everyone has the right to life, liberty and the security of person.

Article 4

No one shall be held in slavery or servitude; slavery and the slave trade shall be prohibited in all their forms.

Article 5

No one shall be subjected to torture or to cruel, inhuman or degrading treatment or punishment.

Article 6

Everyone has the right to recognition everywhere as a person before the law.

Article 7

All are equal before the law and are entitled without any discrimination to equal protection of the law. All are entitled to equal protection against any discrimination in violation of this Declaration and against any incitement to such discrimination.

Article 8

Everyone has the right to an effective remedy by the competent national tribunals for acts violating the fundamental rights granted him by the constitution or by law.

Article 9

No one shall be subjected to arbitrary arrest, detention or exile.

Article 10

Everyone is entitled in full equality to a fair and public hearing by an independent and impartial tribunal, in the determination of his rights and obligations and of any criminal charge against him.

Article 11

1. Everyone charged with a penal offence has the right to be presumed innocent until proved guilty according to law in a public trial at which he has had all the guarantees necessary for his defence.

2. No one shall be held guilty of any penal offence on account of any act or omission which did not constitute a penal offence, under national or international law, at the time when it was committed. Nor shall a heavier penalty be imposed than the one that was applicable at the time the penal offence was committed.

Article 12

No one shall be subjected to arbitrary interference with his privacy, family, home or correspondence, nor to attacks upon his honour and reputation. Everyone has the right to the protection of the law against such interference or attacks.

Article 13

1. Everyone has the right to freedom of movement and residence within the borders of each State.

2. Everyone has the right to leave any country, including his own, and to return to his country.

Article 14

1. Everyone has the right to seek and to enjoy in other countries asylum from persecution.

2. This right may not be invoked in the case of prosecutions genuinely arising from non-political crimes or from acts contrary to the purposes and principles of the United Nations.

Article 15

1. Everyone has the right to a nationality.

2. No one shall be arbitrarily deprived of his nationality nor denied the right to change his nationality.

Article 16

1. Men and women of full age, without any limitation due to race, nationality or religion, have the right to marry and to found a family. They are entitled to equal rights as to marriage, during marriage and at its dissolution.

2. Marriage shall be entered into only with the free and full consent of the intending spouses.

3. The family is the natural and fundamental group unit of society and is entitled to protection by society and the State.

Article 17

1. Everyone has the right to own property alone as well as in association with others.

2. No one shall be arbitrarily deprived of his property.

Article 18

Everyone has the right to freedom of thought, conscience and religion; this right includes freedom to change his religion or belief, and freedom, either alone or in community with others and in public or private, to manifest his religion or belief in teaching, practice, worship and observance.

Article 19

Everyone has the right to freedom of opinion and expression; this right includes freedom to hold opinions without interference and to seek, receive and impart information and ideas through any media and regardless of frontiers.

Article 20

1. Everyone has the right to freedom of peaceful assembly and association.

2. No one may be compelled to belong to an association.

Article 21

1. Everyone has the right to take part in the government of his country, directly or through freely chosen representatives.

2. Everyone has the right of equal access to public service in his country.

3. The will of the people shall be the basis of the authority of government; this will shall be expressed in periodic and genuine elections which shall be by universal and equal suffrage and shall be held by secret vote or by equivalent free voting procedures.

Article 22

Everyone, as a member of society, has the right to social security and is entitled to realization, through national effort and international cooperation and in accordance with the organization and resources of each State, of the economic, social and cultural rights indispensable for his dignity and the free development of his personality.

Article 23

1. Everyone has the right to work, to free choice of employment, to just and favourable conditions of work and to protection against unemployment.

2. Everyone, without any discrimination, has the right to equal pay for equal work.

3. Everyone who works has the right to just and favourable remuneration ensuring for himself and his family an existence worthy of human dignity, and supplemented, if necessary, by other means of social protection.

4. Everyone has the right to form and to join trade unions for the protection of his interests.

Article 24

Everyone has the right to rest and leisure, including reasonable limitation of working hours and periodic holidays with pay.

Article 25

1. Everyone has the right to a standard of living adequate for the health and well-being of himself and of his family, including food, clothing, housing and medical care and necessary social services, and the right to security in the event of unemployment, sickness, disability, widowhood, old age or other lack of livelihood in circumstances beyond his control.

2. Motherhood and childhood are entitled to special care and assistance. All children, whether born in or out of wedlock, shall enjoy the same social protection.

Article 26

1. Everyone has the right to education. Education shall be free, at least in the elementary and fundamental stages. Elementary education shall be compulsory. Technical and professional education shall be made generally available and higher education shall be equally accessible to all on the basis of merit.

2. Education shall be directed to the full development of the human personality and to the strengthening of respect for human rights and fundamental freedoms. It shall promote understanding, tolerance and friendship among all nations, racial or religious groups, and shall further the activities of the United Nations for the maintenance of peace.

3. Parents have a prior right to choose the kind of education that shall be given to their children.

Article 27

1. Everyone has the right freely to participate in the cultural life of the community, to enjoy the arts and to share in scientific advancement and its benefits.

2. Everyone has the right to the protection of the moral and material interests resulting from any scientific, literary or artistic production of which he is the author.

Article 28

Everyone is entitled to a social and international order in which the rights and freedoms set forth in this Declaration can be fully realized.

Article 29

1. Everyone has duties to the community in which alone the free and full development of his personality is possible.

2. In the exercise of his rights and freedoms, everyone shall be subject only to such limitations as are determined by law solely for the purpose of securing due recognition and respect for the rights and freedoms of others and of meeting the just requirements of morality, public order and the general welfare in a democratic society.

3. These rights and freedoms may in no case be exercised contrary to the purposes and principles of the United Nations.

Article 30

Nothing in this Declaration may be interpreted as implying for any State, group or person any right to engage in any activity or to perform any act aimed at the destruction of any of the rights and freedoms set forth herein.

2. INTERNATIONAL COVENANT ON ECONOMIC, SOCIAL AND CULTURAL RIGHTS

PREAMBLE

The State Parties to the present Covenant,

Considering that, in accordance with the principles proclaimed in the Charter of the United Nations, recognition of the inherent dignity and of the equal and inalienable rights of all the members of the human family is the foundation of freedom, justice and peace in the world,

Recognizing that these rights derive from the inherent dignity of the human person,

Recognizing that, in accordance with the Universal Declaration of Human Rights, the ideal of free human beings enjoying freedom from fear and want can only be achieved if conditions are created whereby everyone may enjoy his economic, social and cultural rights, as well as his civil and political rights,

Considering the obligation of States under the Charter of the United Nations to promote universal respect for, and observance of, human rights and freedoms,

Realizing that the individual, having duties to other individuals and to the community to which he belongs, is under a responsibility to strive for the promotion and observance of the rights recognized in the present Covenant,

Agree upon the following articles:

PART I

Article 1

1. All peoples have the right of self-determination. By virtue of that right they freely determine their political status and freely pursue their economic, social and cultural development.

2. All peoples may, for their own ends, freely dispose of their natural wealth and resources without prejudice to any obligations arising out of international economic cooperation, based upon the principle of mutual benefit, and international law. In no case may a people be deprived of its own means of subsistence.

3. The States Parties to the present Covenant, including those having responsibility for the administration of Non-Self-Governing and Trust Territories, shall promote the realization of the right of self-determination, and shall respect that right, in conformity with the provisions of the Charter of the United Nations.

PART II

Article 2

1. Each State Party to the present Covenant undertakes to take steps, individually and through international assistance and cooperation, especially economic and technical, to the maximum of its available resources, with a view to achieving progressively the full realization of the rights recognized in the present Covenant by all appropriate means, including particularly the adoption of legislative measures.

2. The States Parties to the present Covenant undertake to guarantee that the rights enunciated in the present Covenant will be exercised without discrimination of any kind as to race, colour, sex, language, religion, political or other opinion, national or social origin, property, birth or other status.

3. Developing countries, with due regard to human rights and their national economy, may determine to what extent they would guarantee the economic rights recognized in the present Covenant to non-nationals.

Article 3

The States Parties to the present Covenant undertake to ensure the equal right of men and women to the enjoyment of all economic, social and cultural rights set forth in the present Covenant.

Article 4

The States Parties to the present Covenant recognize that, in the enjoyment of those rights provided by the State in conformity with the present Covenant, the State may subject such rights only to such limitations as are determined by law only in so far as this may be compatible with the nature of these rights and solely for the purpose of promoting the general welfare in a democratic society.

Article 5

1. Nothing in the present Covenant may be interpreted as implying for any State, group or person any right to engage in any activity or to perform any act aimed at the destruction of any of the rights or freedoms recognized herein, or at their limitation to a greater extent than is provided for in the present Covenant.

2. No restriction upon or derogation from any of the fundamental human rights recognized or existing in any country in virtue of law, conventions, regulations or custom shall be admitted on the pretext that the present Covenant does not recognize such rights or that it recognizes them to a lesser extent.

PART III

Article 6

1. The States Parties to the present Covenant recognize the right to work, which includes the right of everyone to the opportunity to gain his living by work which he freely chooses or accepts, and will take appropriate steps to safeguard this right.

2. The steps to be taken by a State Party to the present Covenant to achieve the full realization of this right shall include technical and vocational guidance and training programmes, policies and techniques to achieve steady economic, social and cultural development and full and productive employment under conditions safeguarding fundamental political and economic freedoms to the individual.

Article 7

The States Parties to the present Covenant recognize the right of everyone to the enjoyment of just and favourable conditions of work which ensure, in particular:

(*a*) Remuneration which provides all workers, as a minimum, with:

(i) Fair wages and equal remuneration for work of equal value without distinction of any kind, in particular women being guaranteed conditions of work not inferior to those enjoyed by men, with equal pay for equal work;

(ii) A decent living for themselves and their families in accordance with the provisions of the present Covenant;

(*b*) Safe and healthy working conditions;

(*c*) Equal opportunity for everyone to be promoted in his employment to an appropriate higher level, subject to no considerations other than those of seniority and competence;

(*d*) Rest, leisure and reasonable limitation of working hours and periodic holidays with pay, as well as remuneration for public holidays.

Article 8

1. The States Parties to the present Covenant undertake to ensure:

(*a*) The right of everyone to form trade unions and join the trade union of his choice, subject only to the rules of the organization concerned, for the promotion and protection of his economic and social interests. No restrictions may be placed on the exercise of this right other than those prescribed by law and which are necessary in a democratic society in the interests of national security or public order or for the protection of the rights and freedoms of others;

(*b*) The right of trade unions to establish national federations or confederations and the right of the latter to form or join international trade-union organizations;

(c) The right of trade unions to function freely subject to no limitations other than those prescribed law and which are necessary in a democratic society in the interests of national security or public order or for the protection of the rights and freedoms of others;

(d) The right to strike, provided that it is exercised in conformity with the laws of the particular country.

2. This article shall not prevent the imposition of lawful restrictions on the exercise of these rights by members of the armed forces or of the police or of the administration of the State.

3. Nothing in this article shall authorize States Parties to the International Labour Organisation Convention of 1948 concerning Freedom of Association and Protection of the Right to Organise to take legislative measures which would prejudice, or apply the law in such a manner as would prejudice, the guarantees provided for in that Convention.

Article 9

The States Parties to the present Covenant recognize the right of everyone to social security, including social insurance.

Article 10

The States Parties to the present covenant recognize that:

1. The widest possible protection and assistance should be accorded to the family, which is the natural and fundamental group unit of society, particularly for its establishment and while it is responsible for the care and education of dependent children. Marriage must be entered into with the free consent of the intending spouses.

2. Special protection should be accorded to mothers during a reasonable period before and after childbirth. During such period working mothers should be accorded paid leave or leave with adequate social security benefits.

3. Special measures of protection and assistance should be taken on behalf of all children and young persons without any discrimination for reasons of parentage or other conditions. Children and young persons should be protected from economic and social exploitation. Their employment in work harmful to their morals or health or dangerous to life or likely to hamper their normal development should be punishable by law. States should also set age limits below which the paid employment of child labour should be prohibited and punishable by law.

Article 11

1. The States Parties to the present Covenant recognize the right of everyone to an adequate standard of living for himself and his family, including adequate food, clothing and housing, and to the continuous improvement of living conditions. The States Parties will take appropriate steps to ensure the realization of this right, recognizing to this effect the essential importance of international cooperation based on free consent.

2. The States Parties to the present Covenant, recognizing the fundamental right of everyone to be free from hunger, shall take, individually and through international cooperation, the measures, including specific programmes, which are needed:

(a) To improve methods of production, conservation and distribution of food by making full use of technical and scientific knowledge, by disseminating knowledge of the principles of nutrition and by developing or reforming agrarian systems in such a way as to achieve the most efficient development and utilization of natural resources;

(b) Taking into account the problems of both food-importing and food-exporting countries, to ensure an equitable distribution of world food supplies in relation to need.

Article 12

1. The States Parties to the present Covenant recognize the right of everyone to the enjoyment of the highest attainable standard of physical and mental health.

2. The steps to be taken by the States Parties to the present Covenant to achieve the full realization of this right shall include those necessary for:

(a) The provision for the reduction of the stillbirth-rate and of infant mortality and for the healthy development of the child;

(b) The improvement of all aspects of environmental and industrial hygiene;

(c) The prevention, treatment and control of epidemic, endemic, occupational and other diseases;

(d) The creation of conditions which would assure to all medical service and medical attention in the event of sickness.

Article 13

1. The States Parties to the present Covenant recognize the right of everyone to education. They agree that education shall be directed to the full development of the human personality and the sense of its dignity, and shall strengthen the respect for human rights and fundamental freedoms. They further agree that education shall enable all persons to participate effectively in a free society, promote understanding, tolerance and friendship among all nations and all racial, ethnic or religious groups, and further the activities of the United Nations for the maintenance of peace.

2. The States Parties to the present Covenant recognize that, with a view to achieving the full realization of this right:

(a) Primary education shall be compulsory and available free to all;

(b) Secondary education in its different forms, including technical and vocational secondary education, shall be made generally available and accessible to all by every appropriate means, and in particular by the progressive introduction of free education;

(c) Higher education shall be made equally accessible to all, on the basis of capacity, by every appropriate means, and in particular by the progressive introduction of free education;

(d) Fundamental education shall be encouraged or intensified as far as possible for those persons who have not received or completed the whole period of their primary education;

(e) The development of a system of schools at all levels shall be actively pursued, an adequate fellowship system shall be established, and the material conditions of teaching staff shall be continuously improved.

3. The States Parties to the present Covenant undertake to have respect for the liberty of parents and, when applicable, legal guardians to choose for their children schools, other than those established by the public authorities, which conform to such minimum educational standards as may be laid down or approved by the State and to ensure the religious and moral education of their children in conformity with their own convictions.

4. No part of this article shall be construed so as to interfere with the liberty of individuals and bodies to establish and direct educational institutions, subject always to the observance of the principles set forth in paragraph 1 of this article and to the requirement that the education given in such institutions shall conform to such minimum standards as may be laid down by the State.

Article 14

Each State Party to the present Covenant which, at the time of becoming a Party, has not been able to secure in its metropolitan territory or other territories under its jurisdiction compulsory primary education, free of charge, undertakes, within two years, to work out and adopt a detailed plan of action for the progressive implementation, within a reasonable number of years, to be fixed in the plan, of the principle of compulsory education free of charge for all.

Article 15

1. The States Parties to the present Covenant recognize the right of everyone:

(a) To take part in cultural life;

(b) To enjoy the benefits of scientific progress and its applications;

(c) To benefit from the protection of the moral and material interests resulting from any scientific, literary or artistic production of which he is the author.

2. The steps to be taken by the States Parties to the present Covenant to achieve the full realization of this right shall include those necessary for the conservation, the development and the diffusion of science and culture.

3. The States Parties to the present Covenant undertake to respect the freedom indispensable for scientific research and creative activity.

4. The States Parties to the present Covenant recognize the benefits to be derived from the encouragement and development of international contacts and cooperation in the scientific and cultural fields.

PART IV

Article 16

1. The States Parties to the present Covenant undertake to submit in conformity with this part of the Covenant reports on the measures which they have adopted and the progress made in achieving the observance of the rights recognized herein.

2. (*a*) All reports shall be submitted to the Secretary-General of the United Nations, who shall transmit copies to the Economic and Social Council for consideration in accordance with the provisions of the present Covenant;

(*b*) The Secretary-General of the United Nations shall also transmit to the specialized agencies copies of the reports, or any relevant parts therefrom, from States Parties to the present Covenant which are also members of these specialized agencies in so far as these reports, or parts therefrom, relate to any matters which fall within the responsibilities of the said agencies in accordance with their constitutional instruments.

Article 17

1. The States Parties to the present Covenant shall furnish their reports in stages, in accordance with a programme to be established by the Economic and Social Council within one year of the entry into force of the present Covenant after consultation with the States Parties and the specialized agencies concerned.

2. Reports may indicate factors and difficulties affecting the degree of fulfilment of obligations under the present Covenant.

3. Where relevant information has previously been furnished to the United Nations or to any specialized agency by any State Party to the present Covenant, it will not be necessary to reproduce that information, but a precise reference to the information so furnished will suffice.

Article 18

Pursuant to its responsibilities under the Charter of the United Nations in the field of human rights and fundamental freedoms, the Economic and Social Council may make arrangements with the specialized agencies in respect of their reporting to it on the progress made in achieving the observance of the provisions of the present covenant falling within the scope of their activities. These reports may include particulars of decisions and recommendations on such implementation adopted by their competent organs.

Article 19

The Economic and Social Council may transmit to the Commission on Human Rights for study and general recommendation or, as appropriate, for information the reports concerning human rights submitted by States in accordance with articles 16 and 17, and those concerning human rights submitted by the specialized agencies in accordance with article 18.

Article 20

The States Parties to the present Covenant and the specialized agencies concerned may submit comments to the Economic and Social Council on any general recommendation under article 19 or reference to such general recommendation in any report of the Commission on Human Rights or any documentation referred to herein.

Article 21

The Economic and Social Council may submit from time to time to the General Assembly reports with recommendations of a general nature and a summary of the information received from the States Parties to the present Covenant and the specialized agencies on the measures taken and the progress made in achieving general observance of the rights recognized in the present Covenant.

Article 22

The Economic and Social Council may bring to the attention of other organs of the United Nations, their subsidiary organs and specialized agencies concerned with furnishing technical assistance any matters arising out of the reports referred to in this part of the present Covenant which may assist such bodies in deciding, each within its field of competence, on the advisability of international measures likely to contribute to the effective progressive implementation of the present Covenant.

Article 23

The States Parties to the present Covenant agree that international action for the achievement of the rights recognized in the present Covenant includes such methods as the conclusion of conventions, the adoption of recommendations, the furnishing of technical assistance and the holding of regional meetings and technical meetings for the purpose of consultation and study organized in conjunction with the Governments concerned.

Article 24

Nothing in the present Covenant shall be interpreted as impairing the provisions of the Charter of the United Nations and of the constitutions of the specialized agencies which define the respective responsibilities of the various organs of the United Nations and of the specialized agencies in regard to the matters dealt with in the present Covenant.

Article 25

Nothing in the present Covenant shall be interpreted as impairing the inherent right of all peoples to enjoy and utilize fully and freely their natural wealth and resources.

PART V

Article 26

1. The present Covenant is open for signature by any State Member of the United Nations or member of any of its specialized agencies, by any State Party to the Statute of the International Court of Justice, and by any other State which has been invited by the General Assembly of the United Nations to become a party to the present Covenant.

2. The present Covenant is subject to ratification. Instruments of ratification shall be deposited with the Secretary-General of the United Nations.

3. The present Covenant shall be open to accession by any State referred to in paragraph 1 of this article.

4. Accession shall be effected by the deposit of an instrument of accession with the Secretary-General of the United Nations.

5. The Secretary-General of the United Nations shall inform all States which have signed the present Covenant or acceded to it of the deposit of each instrument of ratification or accession.

Article 27

1. The present Covenant shall enter into force three months after the date of the deposit with the Secretary-General of the United Nations of the thirty-fifth instrument of ratification or instrument of accession.

2. For each State ratifying the present Covenant or acceding to it after the deposit of the thirty-fifth instrument of ratification or instrument of accession, the present Covenant shall enter into force three months after the date of the deposit of its own instrument of ratification or instrument of accession.

Article 28

The provisions of the present Covenant shall extend to all parts of federal States without any limitations or exceptions.

Article 29

1. Any State Party to the present Covenant may propose an amendment and file it with the Secretary-General of the United Nations. The Secretary-General shall thereupon communicate any pro-

posed amendments to the States Parties to the present Covenant with a request that they notify him whether they favour a conference of States Parties for the purpose of considering and voting upon the proposals. In the event that at least one third of the States Parties favours such a conference, the Secretary-General shall convene the conference under the auspices of the United Nations. Any amendment adopted by a majority of the States Parties present and voting at the conference shall be submitted to the General Assembly of the United Nations for approval.

2. Amendments shall come into force when they have been approved by the General Assembly of the United Nations and accepted by a two-thirds majority of the States Parties to the present Covenant in accordance with their respective constitutional processes.

3. When amendments come into force they shall be binding on those States Parties which have accepted them, other States Parties still being bound by the provisions of the present Covenant and any earlier amendment which they have accepted.

Article 30

Irrespective of the notifications made under article 26, paragraph 5, the Secretary-General of the United Nations shall inform all States referred to in paragraph 1 of the same article of the following particulars:

(*a*) Signatures, ratifications and accessions under article 26;

(*b*) The date of the entry into force of the present Covenant under article 27 and the date of the entry into force of any amendments under article 29.

Article 31

1. The present Covenant, of which the Chinese, English, French, Russian and Spanish texts are equally authentic, shall be deposited in the archives of the United Nations.

2. The Secretary-General of the United Nations shall transmit certified copies of the present Covenant to all States referred to in article 26.

3. INTERNATIONAL COVENANT ON CIVIL AND POLITICAL RIGHTS

PREAMBLE

The States Parties to the present Covenant,

Considering that, in accordance with the principles proclaimed in the Charter of the United Nations, recognition of the inherent dignity and of the equal and inalienable rights of all members of the human family is the foundation of freedom, justice and peace in the world,

Recognizing that these rights derive from the inherent dignity of the human person,

Recognizing that, in accordance with the Universal Declaration of Human Rights, the ideal of free human beings enjoying civil and political freedom and freedom from fear and want can only be achieved if conditions are created whereby everyone may enjoy his civil and political rights, as well as his economic, social and cultural rights,

Considering the obligations of States under the Charter of the United Nations to promote universal respect for, and observance of, human rights and freedoms,

Realizing that the individual, having duties to other individuals and to the community to which he belongs, is under a responsibility to strive for the promotion and observance of the rights recognized in the present Covenant,

Agree upon the following articles:

PART I

Article 1

1. All peoples have the right of self-determination. By virtue of that right they freely determine their political status and freely pursue their economic, social and cultural development.

2. All peoples may, for their own ends, freely dispose of their natural wealth and resources without prejudice to any obligations arising out of international economic cooperation, based upon the principle of mutual benefit, and international law. In no case may a people be deprived of its own means of subsistence.

3. The States Parties to the present Covenant, including those having responsibility for the administration of Non-Self-Governing and trust Territories, shall promote the realization of the right of self-determination, and shall respect that right, in conformity with the provisions of the Charter of the United Nations.

PART II

Article 2

1. Each State Party to the present Covenant undertakes to respect and to ensure to all individuals within its territory and subject to its jurisdiction the rights recognized in the present Covenant, without distinction of any kind, such as race, colour, sex, language, religion, political or other opinion, national or social origin, property, birth or other status.

2. Where not already provided for by existing legislative or other measures, each State Party to the present Covenant undertakes to take the necessary steps, in accordance with its constitutional processes and with the provisions of the present Covenant, to adopt such legislative or other measures as may be necessary to give effect to the rights recognized in the present Covenant.

3. Each State Party to the present covenant undertakes:

(*a*) To ensure that any person whose rights or freedoms as herein recognized are violated shall have an effective remedy, notwithstanding that the violation has been committed by persons acting in an official capacity;

(*b*) To ensure that any person claiming such a remedy shall have his right thereto determined by competent judicial, administrative or legislative authorities, or by any other competent authority provided for by the legal system of the State, and to develop the possibilities of judicial remedy;

(*c*) To ensure that the competent authorities shall enforce such remedies where granted.

Article 3

The States Parties to the present Covenant undertake to ensure the equal right of men and women to the enjoyment of all civil and political rights set forth in the present Covenant.

Article 4

1. In time of public emergency which threatens the life of the nation and the existence of which is officially proclaimed, the States Parties to the present Covenant may take measures derogating from their obligations under the present Covenant to the extent strictly required by the exigencies of the situation, provided that such measures are not inconsistent with their other obligations under international law and do not involve discrimination solely on the ground of race, colour, sex, language, religion or social origin.

2. No derogation from articles 6, 7, 8 (paragraphs 1 and 2), 11, 15, 16 and 18 may be made under this provision.

3. Any State Party to the present Covenant availing itself of the right of derogation shall immediately inform the other States Parties to the present Covenant, through the intermediary of the Secretary-General of the United Nations, of the provisions from which it has derogated and of the reasons by which it was actuated. A further communication shall be made, through the same intermediary, on the date on which it terminates such derogation.

Article 5

1. Nothing in the present Covenant may be interpreted as implying for any State, group or person any right to engage in any activity or perform any act aimed at the destruction of any of the rights and freedoms recognized herein or at their limitation to a greater extent than is provided for in the present Covenant.

2. There shall be no restriction upon or derogation from any of the fundamental human rights recognized or existing in any State Party to the present Covenant pursuant to law, conventions, regulations or custom on the pretext that the present Covenant does not recognize such rights or that it recognizes them to a lesser extent.

PART III

Article 6

1. Every human being has the inherent right to life. This right shall be protected by law. No one shall be arbitrarily deprived of his life.

2. In countries which have not abolished the death penalty, sentence of death may be imposed only for the most serious crimes in accordance with the law in force at the time of the commission of the crime and not contrary to the provisions of the present Covenant and to the convention on the Prevention and Punishment of the Crime of Genocide. This penalty can only be carried out pursuant to a final judgement rendered by a competent court.

3. When deprivation of life constitutes the crime of genocide, it is understood that nothing in this article shall authorize any State Party to the present Covenant to derogate in any way from any obligation assumed under the provisions of the Convention on the Prevention and Punishment of the Crime of Genocide.

4. Anyone sentenced to death shall have the right to seek pardon or commutation of the sentence. Amnesty, pardon or commutation of the sentence of death may be granted in all cases.

5. Sentence of death shall not be imposed for crimes committed by persons below eighteen years of age and shall not be carried out on pregnant women.

6. Nothing in this article shall be invoked to delay or to prevent the abolition of capital punishment by any State Party to the present Covenant.

Article 7

No one shall be subjected to torture or to cruel, inhuman or degrading treatment or punishment. In particular, no one shall be subjected without this free consent to medical or scientific experimentation.

Article 8

1. No one shall be held in slavery; slavery and the slave-trade in all their forms shall be prohibited.

2. No one shall be held in servitude.

3. (a) No one shall be required to perform forced or compulsory labour;

(b) Paragraph 3 (a) shall not be held to preclude, in countries where imprisonment with hard labour may be imposed as a punishment for a crime, the performance of hard labour in pursuance of a sentence to such punishment by a competent court;

(c) For the purpose of this paragraph the term "forced or compulsory labour" shall not include:

(i) Any work or service, not referred to in subparagraph (b), normally required of a person who is under detention in consequence of a lawful order of a court, or of a person during conditional release from such detention;

(ii) Any service of a military character and, in countries where conscientious objection is recognized, any national service required by law of conscientious objectors;

(iii) Any service exacted in cases of emergency or calamity threatening the life or well-being of the community;

(iv) Any work or service which forms part of normal civil obligations.

Article 9

1. Everyone has the right to liberty and security of person. No one shall be subjected to arbitrary arrest or detention. No one shall be deprived of his liberty except on such grounds and in accordance with such procedure as are established by law.

2. Anyone who is arrested shall be informed, at the time of arrest, of the reasons for his arrest and shall be promptly informed of any charges against him.

3. Anyone arrested or detained on a criminal charge shall be brought promptly before a judge or other officer authorized by law to exercise judicial power and shall be entitled to trial within a reasonable time or to release. It shall not be the general rule that persons awaiting trial shall be detained in custody, but release may be subject to guarantees to appear for trial, at any other stage of the judicial proceedings, and, should occasion arise, for execution of the judgement.

4. Anyone who is deprived of his liberty by arrest or detention shall be entitled to take proceedings before a court, in order that that court may decide without delay on the lawfulness of his detention and order his release if the detention is not lawful.

5. Anyone who has been the victim of unlawful arrest or detention shall have an enforceable right to compensation.

Article 10

1. All persons deprived of their liberty shall be treated with humanity and with respect for the inherent dignity of the human person.

2. (a) Accused persons shall, save in exceptional circumstances, be segregated from convicted persons and shall be subject to separate treatment appropriate to their status as unconvicted persons;

(b) Accused juvenile persons shall be separated from adults and brought as speedily as possible for adjudication.

3. The penitentiary system shall comprise treatment of prisoners the essential aim of which shall be their reformation and social rehabilitation. Juvenile offenders shall be segregated from adults and be accorded treatment appropriate to their age and legal status.

Article 11

No one shall be imprisoned merely on the ground of inability to fulfil a contractual obligation.

Article 12

1. Everyone lawfully within the territory of a State shall, within that territory, have the right to liberty of movement and freedom to choose his residence.

2. Everyone shall be free to leave any country, including his own.

3. The above-mentioned rights shall not be subject to any restrictions except those which are provided by law, are necessary to protect national security, public order (ordre public), public health or morals or the rights and freedoms of others, and are consistent with the other rights recognized in the present Covenant.

4. No one shall be arbitrarily deprived of the right to enter his own country.

Article 13

An alien lawfully in the territory of a State Party to the present Covenant may be expelled therefrom only in pursuance of a decision reached in accordance with law and shall, except where compelling reasons of national security otherwise require, be allowed to submit the reasons against his expulsion and to have his case reviewed by, and be represented for the purpose before, the competent authority or a person or persons especially designated by the competent authority.

Article 14

1. All persons shall be equal before the courts and tribunals. In the determination of any criminal charge against him, or of his rights and obligations in a suit at law, everyone shall be entitled to a fair and public hearing by a competent, independent and impartial tribunal established by law. The Press and the public may be excluded from all or part of a trial for reasons of morals, public order (*ordre public*) or national security in democratic society, or when the interest of the private lives of the parties so requires, or to the extent strictly necessary in the opinion of the court in special circumstances where publicity would prejudice the interests of justice; but any judgement rendered in a criminal case or in a suit at law shall be made public except where the interest of juvenile persons otherwise requires or the proceedings concern matrimonial disputes or the guardianship of children.

2. Everyone charged with a criminal offence shall have the right to be presumed innocent until proved guilty according to law.

3. In the determination of any criminal charge against him, everyone shall be entitled to the following minimum guarantees, in full equality:

(*a*) To be informed promptly and in detail in a language which he understands of the nature and cause of the charge against him;

(*b*) To have adequate time and facilities for the preparation of his defence and to communicate with counsel of his own choosing;

(*c*) To be tried without undue delay;

(*d*) To be tried in his presence, and to defend himself in person or through legal assistance of his own choosing; to be informed, if he does not have legal assistance, of this right; and to have legal assistance assigned to him, in any case where the interests of justice so require, and without payment by him in any such case if he does not have sufficient means to pay for it;

(*e*) To examine, or have examined, the witnesses against him and to obtain the attendance and examination of witnesses on his behalf under the same conditions as witnesses against him;

(*f*) To have the free assistance of an interpreter if he cannot understand or speak the language used in court;

(*g*) Not to be compelled to testify against himself or to confess guilt.

4. In the case of juvenile persons, the procedure shall be such as will take account of their age and the desirability of promoting their rehabilitation.

5. Everyone convicted of a crime shall have the right to his conviction and sentence being reviewed by a higher tribunal according to law.

6. When a person has by a final decision been convicted of a criminal offence and when subsequently his conviction has been reversed or he has been pardoned on the ground that a new newly discovered fact shows conclusively that there has been a miscarriage of justice, the person who has suffered punishment as a result of such conviction shall be compensated according to law, unless it is proved that the non-disclosure of the unknown fact in time is wholly or partly attributable to him.

7. No one shall be liable to be tried or punished again for an offence for which he has already been finally convicted or acquitted in accordance with the law and penal procedure of each country.

Article 15

1. No one shall be held guilty of any criminal offence on account of any act or omission which did not constitute a criminal offence, under national or international law, at the time when it was committed. Nor shall a heavier penalty be imposed than the one that was applicable at the time when the criminal offence was committed. If, subsequent to the commission of the offence, provision is made by law for the imposition of a lighter penalty, the offender shall benefit thereby.

2. Nothing in this article shall prejudice the trial and punishment of any person for any act or omission which, at the time when it was committed, was criminal according to the general principles of law recognized by the community of nations.

Article 16

Everyone shall have the right to recognition everywhere as a person before the law.

Article 17

1. No one shall be subjected to arbitrary or unlawful interference with his privacy, family, home or correspondence, nor to unlawful attacks on his honour and reputation.

2. Everyone has the right to the protection of the law against such interference or attacks.

Article 18

1. Everyone shall have the right to freedom of thought, conscience and religion. This right shall include freedom to have or to adopt a religion or belief of his choice, and freedom, either individually or in community with others and in public or private, to manifest his religion or belief in worship, observance, practice and teaching.

2. No one shall be subject to coercion which would impair his freedom to have or to adopt a religion or belief of his choice.

3. Freedom to manifest one's religion or beliefs may be subject only to such limitations as are prescribed by law and are necessary to protect public safety, order, health, or morals or the fundamental rights and freedoms of others.

4. The States Parties to the present Covenant undertake to have respect for the liberty of parents and, when applicable, legal guardians to ensure the religious and moral education of their children in conformity with their own convictions.

Article 19

1. Everyone shall have the right to hold opinions without interference.

2. Everyone shall have the right to freedom of expression; this right shall include freedom to seek, receive and impart information and ideas of all kinds, regardless of frontiers, either orally, in writing or in print, in the form of art, or through any other media of his choice.

3. The exercise of the rights provided for in paragraph 2 of this article carries with it special duties and responsibilities. It may therefore be subject to certain restrictions, but these shall only be such as are provided by law and are necessary:

(*a*) For respect of the rights or reputations of others;

(*b*) For the protection of national security or of public order (*ordre public*), or of public health or morals.

Article 20

1. Any propaganda for war shall be prohibited by law.

2. Any advocacy of national, racial or religious hatred that constitutes incitement to discrimination, hostility or violence shall be prohibited by law.

Article 21

The right of peaceful assembly shall be recognized. No restrictions may be placed on the exercise of this right other than those imposed in conformity with the law and which are necessary in a democratic society in the interests of national security or public safety, public order (*ordre public*), the protection of public health or morals or the protection of the rights and freedoms of others.

Article 22

1. Everyone shall have the right of freedom of association with others, including the right to form and join trade unions for the protection of his interests.

2. No restrictions may be placed on the exercise of this right other than those which are prescribed by law and which are necessary in a democratic society in the interests of national security or public safety, public order (*ordre public*), the protection of public health or morals or the protection of the rights and freedoms of others. This article shall not prevent the imposition of lawful restrictions on members of the armed forces and of the police in their exercise of this right.

3. Nothing in this article shall authorize States Parties to the International Labour Organisation Convention of 1948 concerning Freedom of Association and Protection of the Right to Organise to take legislative measures which would prejudice, or to apply the law in such a manner as to prejudice, the guarantees provided for in that Convention.

Article 23

1. The family is the natural and fundamental group unit of society and is entitled to protection by society and the State.

2. The right of men and women of marriageable age to marry and to found a family shall be recognized.

3. No marriage shall be entered into without the free and full consent of the intending spouses.

4. States Parties to the present Covenant shall take appropriate steps to ensure equality of rights and responsibilities of spouses as to marriage, during marriage and at its dissolution. In the case of dissolution, provision shall be made for the necessary protection of any children.

Article 24

1. Every child shall have, without any discrimination as to race, colour, sex, language, religion, national or social origin, property or birth, the right to such measures of protection as are required by his status as a minor, on the part of his family, society and the State.

2. Every child shall be registered immediately after birth and shall have a name.

3. Every child has the right to acquire a nationality.

Article 25

Every citizen shall have the right and the opportunity, without any of the distinctions mentioned in article 2 and without unreasonable restrictions:

(*a*) To take part in the conduct of public affairs, directly or through freely chosen representatives;

(*b*) To vote and to be elected at genuine periodic elections which shall be by universal and equal suffrage and shall be held by secret ballot, guaranteeing the free expression of the will of the electors;

(*c*) To have access, on general terms of equality, to public service in his country.

Article 26

All persons are equal before the law and are entitled without any discrimination to the equal protection of the law. In this respect, the law shall prohibit any discrimination and guarantee to all persons equal and effective protection against discrimination on any ground such as race, colour, sex, language, religion, political or other opinion, national or social origin, property, birth or other status.

Article 27

In those States in which ethnic, religious or linguistic minorities exist, persons belonging to such minorities shall not be denied the right, in community with the other members of their group, to enjoy their own culture, to profess and practise their own religion, or to use their own language.

PART IV

Article 28

1. There shall be established a Human Rights Committee (hereafter referred to in the present Covenant as the Committee). It shall consist of eighteen members and shall carry out the functions hereinafter provided.

2. The Committee shall be composed of nationals of the States Parties to the present Covenant who shall be persons of high moral character and recognized competence in the field of human rights, consideration being given to the usefulness of the participation of some persons having legal experience.

3. The members of the Committee shall be elected and shall serve in their personal capacity.

Article 29

1. The members of the Committee shall be elected by secret ballot from a list of persons possessing the qualifications prescribed in article 28 and nominated for the purpose by the States Parties to the present Covenant.

2. Each State Party to the present Covenant may nominate not more than two persons. These persons shall be nationals of the nominating State.

3. A person shall be eligible for renomination.

Article 30

1. The initial election shall be held no later than six months after the date of the entry into force of the present Covenant.

2. At least four months before the date of each election to the Committee, other than an election to fill a vacancy declared in accordance with article 34, the Secretary-General of the United Nations shall address a written invitation to the States Parties to the present Covenant to submit their nominations for membership of the Committee within three months.

3. The Secretary-General of the United Nations shall prepare a list in alphabetical order of all the persons thus nominated, with an indication of the States Parties which have nominated them, and shall submit it to the States Parties to the present Covenant no later than one month before the date of each election.

4. Elections of the members of the Committee shall be held at a meeting of the States Parties to the present Covenant convened by the Secretary-General of the United Nations at the Headquarters of the United Nations. At that meeting, for which two thirds of the States Parties to the present Covenant shall constitute a quorum, the persons elected to the Committee shall be those nominees who obtain the largest number of votes and an absolute majority of the votes of the representatives of States Parties present and voting.

Article 31

1. The Committee may not include more than one national of the same State.

2. In the election of the Committee, consideration shall be given to equitable geographical distribution of membership and to the representation of the different forms of civilization and of the principal legal systems.

Article 32

1. The members of the Committee shall be elected for a term of four years. They shall be eligible for reelection if renominated. However the terms of nine of the members elected at the first election shall expire at the end of two years; immediately after the first election, the names of these nine members shall be chosen by lot by the Chairman of the meeting referred to in article 30, paragraph 4.

2. Elections at the expiry of office shall be held in accordance with the preceding articles of this part of the present Covenant.

Article 33

1. If, in the unanimous opinion of the other members, a member of the Committee has ceased to carry out his functions for any cause other than absence of a temporary character, the Chairman of the Committee shall notify the Secretary-General of the United Nations who shall then declare the seat of that member to be vacant.

2. In the event of the death or the resignation of a member of the Committee, the Chairman shall immediately notify the Secretary-

General of the United Nations, who shall declare the seat vacant from the date of death or the date on which the resignation takes effect.

Article 34

1. When a vacancy is declared in accordance with article 33 and if the term of office of the member to be replaced does not expire within six months of the declaration of the vacancy, the Secretary-General of the United Nations shall notify each of the States Parties to the present Covenant, which may within two months submit nominations in accordance with article 29 for the purpose of filling the vacancy.

2. The Secretary-General of the United Nations shall prepare a list in alphabetical order of the person thus nominated and shall submit it to the States Parties of the present Covenant. The election to fill the vacancy shall then take place in accordance with the relevant provisions of this part of the present Covenant.

3. A member of the Committee elected to fill a vacancy declared in accordance with article 33 shall hold office for the remainder of the term of the member who vacated the seat on the Committee under the provisions of that article.

Article 35

The members of the Committee shall, with the approval of the General Assembly of the United Nations, receive emoluments from United Nations resources on such terms and conditions as the General Assembly may decide, having regard to the importance of the Committee's responsibilities.

Article 36

The Secretary-General of the United Nations shall provide the necessary staff and facilities for the effective performance of the functions of the Committee under the present Covenant.

Article 37

1. The Secretary-General of the United Nations shall convene the initial meeting of the Committee at the Headquarters of the United Nations.

2. After its initial meeting, the Committee shall meet at such times as shall be provided in its rules of procedure.

3. The Committee shall normally meet at the Headquarters of the United Nations or at the United Nations Office at Geneva.

Article 38

Every member of the committee shall, before taking up his duties, make a solemn declaration in open committee that he will perform his functions impartially and conscientiously.

Article 39

1. The Committee shall elect its officers for a term of two years. They may be re-elected.

2. The Committee shall establish its own rules of procedure, but these rules shall provide, *inter alia*, that:

(a) Twelve members shall constitute a quorum;

(b) Deecisions of the Committee shall be made by a majority vote of the members present.

Article 40

1. The States Parties to the present Covenant undertake to submit reports on the measures they have adopted which give effect to the rights recognized herein and on the progress made in the enjoyment of those rights:

(a) Within one year of the entry into force of the present Covenant for the States Parties concerned;

(b) Thereafter whenever the Committee so requests.

2. All reports shall be submitted to the Secretary-General of the United Nations, who shall transmit them to the Committee for consideration. Reports shall indicate the factors and difficulties, if any, affecting the implementation of the present Covenant.

3. The Secretary-General of the United Nations may, after consultation with the Committee, transmit to the specialized agencies concerned copies of such parts of the reports as may fall within their field of competence.

4. The Committee shall study the reports submitted by the States Parties to the present Covenant. It shall transmit its reports, and such general comments as it may consider appropriate, to the States Parties. The Committee may also transmit to the Economic and Social Council these comments along with the copies of the reports it has received from States Parties to the present Covenant.

5. The States Parties to the present Covenant may submit to the Committee observations on any comments that may be made in accordance with paragraph 4 of this article.

Article 41

1. A State Party to the present Covenant may at any time declare under this article that it recognizes the competence of the committee to receive and consider communications to the effect that a State Party claims that another State Party is not fulfilling its obligations under the present Covenant. Communications under this article may be received and considered only if submitted by a State Party which has made a declaration recognizing in regard to itself the competence of the Committee. No communication shall be received by the Committee if it concerns a State Party which has not made such a declaration. Communications received under this article shall be dealt with in accordance with the following procedure:

(a) If a State Party to the present Covenant considers that another State Party is not giving effect to the provisions of the present Covenant, it may, by written communication, bring the matter to the attention of that State Party. Within three months after the receipt of the communication, the receiving State shall afford the State which sent the communication an explanation or any other statement in writing clarifying the matter, which should include, to the extent possible and pertinent, reference to domestic procedures and remedies taken, pending, or available in the matter.

(b) If the matter is not adjusted to the satisfaction of both States Parties concerned within six months after the receipt by the receiving State of the initial communication, either State shall have the right to refer the matter to the Committee, by notice given to the Committee and to the other State.

(c) The committee shall deal with a matter referred to it only after it has ascertained that all available domestic remedies have been invoked and exhausted in the matter, in conformity with the generally recognized principles of international law. This shall not be the rule where the application of the remedies is unreasonably prolonged.

(d) The Committee shall hold closed meetings when examining communications under this article.

(e) Subject to the provisions of subparagraph (c), the Committee shall make available its good offices to the States Parties concerned with a view to a friendly solution of the matter on the basis of respect for human rights and fundamental freedoms as recognized in the present Covenant.

(f) In any matter referred to it, the Committee may call upon the States Parties concerned, referred to in subparagraph (b), to supply any relevant information.

(g) The States Parties concerned, referred to in subparagraph (b), shall have the right to be represented when the matter is being considered in the Committee and to make submissions orally and/or in writing.

(h) The Committee shall, within twelve months after the date of receipt of notice under subparagraph (b), submit a report:

(i) If a solution within the terms of subparagraph (e) is reached, the Committee shall confine its reports to a brief statement of the facts and of the solution reached;

(ii) If a solution within the terms of subparagraph (e) is not reached, the committee shall confine its report to a brief statement of the facts; the written submissions and record of the oral submissions made by the States Parties concerned shall be attached to the report.

In every matter, the report shall be communicated to the States Parties concerned.

2. The provisions of this article shall come into come force when ten States Parties to the present Covenant have made declarations under paragraph 1 of this article. Such declarations shall be deposited by the States Parties with the Secretary-General of the United Nations, who shall transmit copies thereof to the other States Parties. A declaration may be withdrawn at any time by notification to the Secretary-General. Such a withdrawal shall not prejudice the consideration of

any matter which is the subject of a communication already transmitted under this article; no further communication by any State Party shall be received after the notification of withdrawal of the Declaration has been received by the Secretary-General, unless the State Party concerned has made a new decision.

Article 42

1. (a) If a matter referred to the Committee in accordance with article 41 is not resolved to the satisfaction of the States Parties concerned, the Committee may, with the prior consent of the States Parties concerned, appoint an *ad hoc* Conciliation Commission (hereinafter referred to as the Commission). The good offices of the Commission shall be made available to the States Parties concerned with a view to an amicable solution of the matter on the basis of respect for the present Covenant;

(b) The Commission shall consist of five persons acceptable to the States Parties concerned. If the States Parties concerned fail to reach agreement within three months on all or part of the composition of the Commission, the members of the Commission concerning whom no agreement has been reached shall be elected by secret ballot by a two-thirds majority vote of the Committee from among its members.

2. The members of the Commission shall serve in their personal capacity. They shall not be nationals of the States Parties concerned, or of a State not party to the present Covenant, or of a State Party which has not made a declaration under article 41.

3. The Commission shall elect its own Chairman and adopt its own rules of procedure.

4. The meetings of the Commission shall normally be held at the Headquarters of the United Nations or at the United Nations Office at Geneva. However, they may be held at such other convenient places as the Commission may determine in consultation with the Secretary-General of the United Nations and the States Parties concerned.

5. The secretariat provided in accordance with article 36 shall also service the commissions appointed under this article.

6. The information received and collated by the Committee shall be made available to the Commission and the Commission may call upon the States Parties concerned to supply any other relevant information.

7. When the Commission has fully considered the matter, but in any event not later than twelve months after having been seized of the matter, it shall submit to the Chairman of the Committee a report for communication to the States Parties concerned:

(a) If the Commission is unable to complete its consideration of the matter within twelve months, it shall confine its report to a brief statement of the status of its consideration of the matter;

(b) If an amicable solution to the matter on the basis of respect for human rights as recognized in the present Covenant is reached, the Commission shall confine its report to a brief statement of the facts and of the solution reached;

(c) If a solution within the terms of subparagraph (b) is not reached, the Commission's report shall embody its findings on all questions of fact relevant to the issues between the States Parties concerned, and its views on the possibilities of an amicable solution of the matter. This report shall also contain the written submissions and a record of the oral submissions made by the States Parties concerned;

(d) If the Commission's report is submitted under subparagraph (c), the States Parties concerned shall, within three months of the receipt of the report, notify the Chairman of the Committee whether or not they accept the contents of the report of the Commission.

8. The provisions of this article are without prejudice to the responsibilities of the Committee under article 41.

9. The States Parties concerned shall share equally all the expenses of the members of the Commission in accordance with estimates to be provided by the Secretary-General of the United Nations.

10. The Secretary-General of the United Nations shall be empowered to pay the expenses of the members of the Commission, if necessary, before reimbursement by the States Parties concerned, in accordance with paragraph 9 of this article.

Article 43

The members of the Committee, and of the *ad hoc* conciliation commissions which may be appointed under article 42, shall be entitled to the facilities, privileges and immunities of experts on mission for the United Nations as laid down in the relevant sections of the Convention on the Privileges and Immunities of the United Nations.

Article 44

The provisions for the implementation of the present Covenant shall apply without prejudice to the procedures prescribed in the field of human rights by or under the constituent instruments and the conventions of the United Nations and of the specialized agencies and shall not prevent the States Parties to the present Covenant from having recourse to other procedures for settling a dispute in accordance with general or special international agreements in force between them.

Article 45

The Committee shall submit to the general Assembly of the United Nations, through the Economic and Social Council, an annual report on its activities.

PART V

Article 46

Nothing in the present Covenant shall be interpreted as impairing the provisions of the Charter of the United Nations and of the constitutions of the specialized agencies which define the respective responsibilities of the various organs of the United Nations and of the specialized agencies in regard to the matters dealt with in the present Covenant.

Article 47

Nothing in the present Covenant shall be interpreted as impairing the inherent right of all peoples to enjoy and utilize fully and freely their natural wealth and resources.

PART VI

Article 48

1. The present Covenant is open for signature by any State Member of the United Nations or member of any of its specialized agencies, by any State Party to the Statute of the International Court of Justice, and by any other State which has been invited by the General Assembly of the United Nations to become a party to the present Covenant.

2. The present Covenant is subject to ratification. Instruments of ratification shall be deposited with the Secretary-General of the United Nations.

3. The present Covenant shall be open to accession by any State referred to in paragraph 1 of this article.

4. Accession shall be effected by the deposit of an instrument of accession with the Secretary-General of the United Nations.

5. The Secretary-General of the United Nations shall inform all States which have signed this Covenant or acceded to it of the deposit of each instrument of ratification or accession.

Article 49

1. The present Covenant shall enter into force three months after the date of the deposit with the Secretary-General of the United Nations of the thirty-fifth instrument of ratification or instrument of accession.

2. For each State ratifying the present Covenant or acceding to it after the deposit of the thirty-fifth instrument of ratification or instrument of accession, the present Covenant shall enter into force three months after the date of the deposit of its own instrument of ratification or instrument of accession.

Article 50

The provisions of the present Covenant shall extend to all parts of federal States without any limitations or exceptions.

Article 51

1. Any State Party to the present Covenant may propose an amendment and file it with the Secretary-General of the United Nations. The Secretary-General of the United Nations shall thereupon

communicate any proposed amendments to the States Parties to the present Covenant with a request that they notify him whether they favour a conference of States Parties for the purpose of considering and voting upon the proposals. In the event that at least one third of the States Parties favours such a conference, the Secretary-General shall convene the conference under the auspices of the United Nations. Any amendment adopted by a majority of the States Parties present and voting at the conference shall be submitted to the General Assembly of the United Nations for approval.

2. Amendments shall come into force when they have been approved by the General Assembly of the United Nations and accepted by a two-thirds majority of the States Parties to the present Covenant in accordance with their respective constitutional processes.

3. When amendments come into force, they shall be binding on those States Parties which have accepted them, other States Parties still being bound by the provisions of the present Covenant and any earlier amendment which they have accepted.

Article 52

Irrespective of the notifications made under article 48, paragraph 5, the Secretary-General of the United Nations shall inform all States referred to in paragraph 1 of the same article of the following particulars:

(a) Signatures, ratifications and accessions under article 48;

(b) The date of the entry into force of the present Covenant under article 49 and the date of the entry into force of any amendments under article 51.

Article 53

1. The present Covenant, of which the Chinese, English, French, Russian and Spanish texts are equally authentic, shall be deposited in the archives of the United Nations.

2. The Secretary-General of the United Nations shall transmit certified copies of the present Covenant to all States referred to in article 48.

4. OPTIONAL PROTOCOL TO THE INTERNATIONAL COVENANT ON CIVIL AND POLITICAL RIGHTS

The States Parties to the present Protocol,

Considering that in order further to achieve the purposes of the Covenant on Civil and Political Rights (hereinafter referred to as the Covenant) and the implementation of its provisions it would be appropriate to enable the Human Rights Committee set up in part IV of the Covenant (hereinafter referred to as the Committee) to receive and consider, as provided in the present Protocol, communications from individuals claiming to be victims of violations of any of the rights set forth in the Covenant,

Have agreed as follows:

Article 1

A State Party to the Covenant that becomes a party to the present Protocol recognizes the competence of the Committee to receive and consider communications from individuals subject to its jurisdiction who claim to be victims of a violation by that State Party of any of the rights set forth in the Covenant. No communication shall be received by the Committee if it concerns a State Party to the Covenant which is not a party to the present Protocol.

Article 2

Subject to the provisions of article 1, individuals who claim that any of their rights enumerated in the Covenant have been violated and who have exhausted all available domestic remedies may submit a written communication to the Committee for consideration.

Article 3

The Committee shall consider inadmissible any communication under the present Protocol which is anonymous, or which it considers to be an abuse of the right of submission of such communications or to be incompatible with the provisions of the Covenant.

Article 4

1. Subject to the provisions of article 3, the Committee shall bring any communications submitted to it under the present Protocol to the attention of the State Party to the present Protocol alleged to be violating any provision of the Covenant.

2. Within six months, the receiving State shall submit to the Committee written explanations or statements clarifying the matter and the remedy, if any, that may have been taken by that State.

Article 5

1. The Committee shall consider communications received under the present Protocol in the light of all written information made available to it by the individual and by the State Party concerned.

2. The Committee shall not consider any communication from an individual unless it has ascertained that:

(a) The same matter is not being examined under another procedure of international investigation or settlement;

(b) The individual has exhausted all available domestic remedies.

This shall not be the rule where the application of the remedies is unreasonably prolonged.

3. The Committee shall hold closed meetings when examining communications under the present Protocol.

4. The Committee shall forward its views to the State Party concerned and to the individual.

Article 6

The Committee shall include in its annual report under article 45 of the Covenant a summary of its activities under the present Protocol.

Article 7

Pending the achievement of the objectives of resolution 1514 (XV) adopted by the General Assembly of the United Nations on 14 December 1960 concerning the Declaration on the Granting of Independence to Colonial Countries and Peoples, the provisions of the present Protocol shall in no way limit the right of petition granted to these peoples by the Charter of the United Nations and other international conventions and instruments under the United Nations and its specialized agencies.

Article 8

1. The present Protocol is open for signature by any State which has signed the Covenant.

2. The present Protocol is subject to ratification by any State which has ratified or acceded to the Covenant. Instruments of ratification shall be deposited with the Secretary-General of the United Nations.

3. The present Protocol shall be open to accession by any State which has ratified or acceded to the Covenant.

4. Accession shall be effected by the deposit of an instrument of accession with the Secretary-General of the United Nations.

5. The Secretary-General of the United Nations shall inform all States which have signed the present Protocol or acceded to it of the deposit of each instrument of ratification or accession.

Article 9

1. Subject to the entry into force of the Covenant, the present Protocol shall enter into force three months after the date of the deposit with the Secretary-General of the United Nations of the tenth instrument of ratification or instrument of accession.

2. For each State ratifying the present Protocol or acceding to it after the deposit of the tenth instrument of ratification or instrument of accession, the present Protocol shall enter into force three months after the date of the deposit of its own instrument of ratification or instrument of accession.

Article 10

The provisions of the present Protocol shall extend to all parts of federal States without any limitations or exceptions.

Article 11

1. Any State Party to the present Protocol may propose an amendment and file it with the Secretary-General of the United Nations. The Secretary-General shall thereupon communicate any proposed amendments to the States Parties to the present Protocol with a request that they notify him whether they favour a conference of States Parties for the purpose of considering and voting upon the proposal. In the event that at least one third of the States Parties favours such a conference, the Secretary-General shall convene the conference under the auspices of the United Nations. Any amendment adopted by a majority of the States Parties present and voting at the conference shall be submitted to the General Assembly of the United Nations for approval.

2. Amendments shall come into force when they have been approved by the General Assembly of the United Nations and accepted by a two-thirds majority of the States Parties to the present Protocol in accordance with their respective constitutional processes.

3. When amendments come into force, they shall be binding on those States Parties which have accepted them, other States Parties still being bound by the provisions of the present Protocol and any earlier amendment which they have accepted.

Article 12

1. Any State Party may denounce the present Protocol at any time by written notification addressed to the Secretary-General of the United Nations. Denunciation shall take effect three months after the date of receipt of the notification by the Secretary-General.

2. Denunciation shall be without prejudice to the continued application of the provisions of the present Protocol to any communication submitted under article 2 before the effective date of denunciation.

Article 13

Irrespective of the notifications made under article 8, paragraph 5, of the present Protocol, the Secretary-General of the United Nations shall inform all States referred to in article 48, paragraph 1, of the Covenant of the following particulars:

(a) Signatures, ratifications and accessions under article 8;

(b) The date of the entry into force of the present Protocol under article 9 and the date of the entry into force of any amendments under article 11;

(c) Denunciations under article 12.

Article 14

1. The present Protocol, of which the Chinese, English, French, Russian and Spanish texts are equally authentic, shall be deposited in the archives of the United Nations.

2. The Secretary-General of the United Nations shall transmit certified copies of the present Protocol to all States referred to in article 48 of the Covenant.

---

5. SECOND OPTIONAL PROTOCOL TO THE INTERNATIONAL COVENANT ON CIVIL AND POLITICAL RIGHTS, AIMING AT THE ABOLITION OF THE DEATH PENALTY

The States Parties to the present Protocol,

Believing that abolition of the death penalty contributes to enhancement of human dignity and progressive development of human rights,

Recalling article 3 of the Universal Declaration of Human Rights, adopted on 10 December 1948, and article 6 of the International Covenant on Civil and Political Rights, adopted on 16 December 1966,

Noting that article 6 of the International Covenant on Civil and Political Rights refers to abolition of the death penalty in terms that strongly suggest that abolition is desirable,

Convinced that all measures of abolition of the death penalty should be considered as progress in the enjoyment of the right to life,

Desirous to undertake hereby an international commitment to abolish the death penalty,

Have agreed as follows:

Article 1

1. No one within the jurisdiction of a State Party to the present Protocol shall be executed.

2. Each State Party shall take all necessary measures to abolish the death penalty within its jurisdiction.

Article 2

1. No reservation is admissible to the present Protocol, except for a reservation made at the time of ratification or accession that provides for the application of the death penalty in time of war pursuant to a conviction for a most serious crime of a military nature committed during wartime.

2. The State Party making such a reservation shall at the time of ratification or accession communicate to the Secretary-General of the United Nations the relevant provisions of its national legislation applicable during wartime.

3. The State Party having made such a reservation shall notify the Secretary-General of the United Nations of any beginning or ending of a state of war applicable to its territory.

Article 3

The States Parties to the present Protocol shall include in the reports they submit to the Human Rights Committee, in accordance with article 40 of the Covenant, information on the measures that they have adopted to give effect to the present Protocol.

Article 4

With respect to the States Parties to the Covenant that have made a declaration under article 41, the competence of the Human Rights Committee to receive and consider communications when a State Party claims that another States Party is not fulfilling its obligations shall extend to the provisions of the present Protocol, unless the State Party concerned has made a statement to the contrary at the moment of ratification or accession.

Article 5

With respect to the States Parties to the first Optional Protocol to the International Covenant on Civil and Political Rights adopted on

16 December 1966, the competence of the Human Rights Committee to receive and consider communications from individuals subject to its jurisdiction shall extend to the provisions of the present Protocol, unless the State Party concerned has made a statement to the contrary at the moment of ratification or accession.

Article 6

1. The provisions of the present Protocol shall apply as additional provisions to the Covenant.

2. Without prejudice to the possibility of a reservation under article 2 of the present Protocol, the right guaranteed in article 1, paragraph 1, of the present Protocol shall not be subject to any derogation under article 4 of the Covenant.

Article 7

1. The present Protocol is open for signature by any State that has signed the Covenant.

2. The present Protocol is subject to ratification by any State that has ratified the Covenant or acceded to it. Instruments of ratification shall be deposited with the Secretary-General of the United Nations.

3. The present Protocol shall be open to accession by any State that has ratified the Covenant or acceded to it.

4. Accession shall be effected by the deposit of an instrument of accession with the Secretary-General of the United Nations.

5. The Secretary-General of the United Nations shall inform all States that have signed the present Protocol or acceded to it of the deposit of each instrument of ratification or accession.

Article 8

1. The present Protocol shall enter into force three months after the date of the deposit with the Secretary-General of the United Nations of the tenth instrument of ratification or accession.

2. For each State ratifying the present Protocol or acceding to it after the deposit of the tenth instrument of ratification or accession, the present Protocol shall enter into force three months after the date of the deposit of its own instrument of ratification or accession.

Article 9

The provisions of the present Protocol shall extend to all parts of federal States without any limitations or exceptions.

Article 10

The Secretary-General of the United Nations shall inform all States referred to in article 48, paragraph 1, of the Covenant of the following particulars:

(a) Reservations, communications and notifications under article 2 of the present Protocol;

(b) Statements made under articles 4 or 5 of the present Protocol;

(c) Signatures, ratifications and accessions under article 7 of the present Protocol;

(d) The date of the entry into force of the present Protocol under article 8 thereof.

Article 11

1. The present Protocol, of which the Arabic, Chinese, English, French, Russian and Spanish texts are equally authentic, shall be deposited in the archives of the United Nations.

2. The Secretary-General of the United Nations shall transmit certified copies of the present Protocol to all States referred to in article 48 of the Covenant.

SELECT BIBLIOGRAPHY[a]

Commonwealth Secretariat. Human Rights Unit. National human rights institutions in the Commonwealth; directory. 2nd ed., rev. Survey and analysis. Comp. and ed. by John Hatchard. London, 1992, 143 p.

—————. Human Rights Unit. National human rights institutions; manual. By John Hatchard. London, 1993, 148 p.

International Ombudsman Institute. Directory of ombudsmen and international ombudsman offices, Edmonton (Alberta), 1992.

United Nations. Centre for Human Rights. National institutions for the promotion and protection of human rights. 1993. 21 p. (Fact Sheet No. 19)

—————. Centre for Human Rights. United Nations workshop for the Asia-Pacific region on human rights issues, Jakarta, 26-28 January 1993; report. 1993. 34 p. (HR/PUB/93/1)

—————. Division of Human Rights. Seminar on national and local institutions for the promotion and protection of human rights, Geneva, 18-29 September 1978. (ST/HR/SER.A/2 and Add.1)

—————. Economic and Social Council. Report of the international workshop on national institutions for the promotion and protection of human rights, Paris, 7-9 October 1991. (E/CN.4/1992/43 and Add.1)

—————. Economic and Social Council. Report of the second international workshop on national institutions for the promotion and protection of human rights, Tunis, 13-17 December 1993. (E/CN.4/1994/45 and Add.1)

—————. Economic and Social Council. Reports of the Secretary-General on national institutions for the promotion and protection of human rights. 1986-1993. (E/CN.4/1987/37; E/CN.4/1989/47 and Add.1; E/CN.4/1991/23 and Add.1; E/CN.4/1993/33)

—————. General Assembly. Report of the meeting of representatives of national institutions and organizations promoting tolerance and harmony and combating racism and racial discrimination, Sydney, 19-23 April 1993. 19 May 1993. 45 p. (A/CONF.157/PC/92/Add.5)

—————. General Assembly. Reports of the Secretary-General on national institutions for the promotion and protection of human rights. 1981-1987. (A/36/440; A/38/416; A/39/556 and Add.1; A/40/469; A/41/464; A/42/395)

---

[a] This bibliography mainly includes items dealing with general issues relating to national human rights institutions. For information regarding particular national institutions, the reader may wish to contact the national institution of the State concerned.